PENGUIN BOOKS

WAKE UP

JACK KEROUAC was born in Lowell, Massachusetts, in 1922 and died in St. Petersburg, Florida, in 1969. His many books include the novels *On the Road*, *The Dharma Bums*, *Visions of Cody*, and *Big Sur*. Kerouac wrote one other book on Buddhism, *Some of the Dharma*, which was completed in 1956 but not published until 1997.

ROBERT THURMAN, chair of religious studies at Columbia University, is the author of many books, including *Inner Revolution: Life, Liberty, and the Pursuit of Real Happiness*; *Infinite Life: Awakening the Bliss Within*; and, most recently, *Why the Dalai Lama Matters: His Act of Truth as the Solution for China, Tibet, and the World.*

ALSO BY JACK KEROUAC

THE DULUOZ LEGEND

Visions of Gerard
Doctor Sax
Maggie Cassidy
Vanity of Duluoz
On the Road
Visions of Cody
The Subterraneans
Tristessa
Lonesome Traveller
Desolation Angels
The Dharma Bums
Book of Dreams
Big Sur
Satori in Paris

POETRY

Mexico City Blues
Scattered Poems
Pomes All Sizes
Heaven and Other Poems
Book of Blues
Book of Haikus
Book of Sketches

OTHER WORK

The Town and the City
*The Scripture of the Golden
   Eternity*
Some of the Dharma
Old Angel Midnight
Good Blonde & Others
Pull My Daisy
Trip Trap
Pic
The Portable Jack Kerouac
Selected Letters: 1940–1956
Selected Letters: 1957–1969
Atop an Underwood
Door Wide Open
Orpheus Emerged
*Departed Angels: The Lost
   Paintings*
Windblown World
Beat Generation: A Play
*On the Road: The Original
   Scroll*

Jack Kerouac, "Enlightenment," pencil in sketchbook, *ca.* 1956

WAKE UP

A Life of the Buddha

Prepared by

JACK KEROUAC

Introduction by Robert A. F. Thurman

PENGUIN BOOKS

PENGUIN BOOKS

Published by the Penguin Group

Penguin Group (USA) Inc., 375 Hudson Street, New York, New York 10014, U.S.A. • Penguin Group
(Canada), 90 Eglinton Avenue East, Suite 700, Toronto, Ontario, Canada M4P 2Y3 (a division of
Pearson Penguin Canada Inc.) • Penguin Books Ltd, 80 Strand, London WC2R 0RL, England •
Penguin Ireland, 25 St Stephen's Green, Dublin 2, Ireland (a division of Penguin Books Ltd) • Penguin
Group (Australia), 250 Camberwell Road, Camberwell, Victoria 3124, Australia (a division of Pearson
Australia Group Pty Ltd) • Penguin Books India Pvt Ltd, 11 Community Centre, Panchsheel Park,
New Delhi – 110 017, India • Penguin Group (NZ), 67 Apollo Drive, Rosedale, North Shore 0632,
New Zealand (a division of Pearson New Zealand Ltd) • Penguin Books (South Africa) (Pty) Ltd, 24
Sturdee Avenue, Rosebank, Johannesburg 2196, South Africa

Penguin Books Ltd, Registered Offices: 80 Strand, London WC2R 0RL, England

First published in the United States of America by Viking Penguin,
a member of Penguin Group (USA) Inc. 2008
Published in Penguin Books 2009

10 9 8 7 6 5 4 3 2 1

Copyright © John Sampas, Literary Representative of the Estate of Jack Kerouac, 2008
Introduction copyright © Robert Thurman, 2008
All rights reserved

Frontispiece: "Enlightenment," a drawing by Jack Kerouac. Henry W. and Albert A. Berg Collection of
English and American Literature, The New York Public Library, Astor, Lenox and Tilden Foundations.

Selections from A Buddhist Bible, edited by Dwight Goddard. Copyright E. P. Dutton & Co., Inc., 1938.
Used by permission of Dutton, a member of Penguin Group (USA) Inc.

CIP data available
ISBN 978-0-670-01957-1 (hc.)
ISBN 978-0-14-311601-1 (pbk.)

Printed in the United States of America
Designed by Carla Bolte • Set in Iowan Oldstyle

Except in the United States of America, this book is sold subject to the condition that it shall not, by
way of trade or otherwise, be lent, resold, hired out, or otherwise circulated without the publisher's
prior consent in any form of binding or cover other than that in which it is published and without a
similar condition including this condition being imposed on the subsequent purchaser.

The scanning, uploading and distribution of this book via the Internet or via any other means without
the permission of the publisher is illegal and punishable by law. Please purchase only authorized
electronic editions, and do not participate in or encourage electronic piracy of copyrighted materials.
Your support of the author's rights is appreciated.

INTRODUCTION

What a surprise! Working on this introduction, it has become apparent to me that Jack Kerouac was the lead bodhisattva, way back there in the 1950s, among all of our very American predecessors. To introduce Kerouac introducing Shakyamuni Buddha, I'm just going to be personal since I'm not a scholar of the Beats and their literature. But Kerouac's interpretation of "beat," that it stands for "beatific" (which is how I like to translate the *sambhoga* of a buddha's *sambhoga-kaya*, "beatific body"—his celestial, universal bliss-form) rather than for "beat up"—those who can't take the industrial slave life, with its productions and its banks and its wars—this won my heart right away. Obviously it did way back when, I just couldn't remember till now.

I am grateful for the opportunity to write this introduction. It has been nearly fifty years since I read *The Dharma Bums*. Now that my love for the Buddhadharma—"the reality of the Enlightened One," "the teaching of the Awakener" (to use not-at-all-bad Kerouac expressions for "Buddha")—has become a bit of a public confession, I am sometimes asked how I came to my interest in it. I tend to mention what I have remembered up to now, that the ground was sown by my reading of Nietszche's *Thus Spake Zarathustra*, Schopenhauer, Kant, Wittgenstein, Henry Miller, Herman Hesse, Freud, Jung, Wilhelm Reich, Lama Govinda, D. T. Suzuki, Evans-Wentz, and so on. I did not remember Kerouac. But I now realize that when I read *The Dharma Bums* as a teen in the late fifties, I was exposed to perhaps the most accurate, poetic, and expansive evocation of the heart of Buddhism that was available at that time. Not to say that it was perfect, or to pretend that I would be able to tell if it was or wasn't—it's just that it is so incredibly inspiring, and must have deeply affected my seventeen-year-old self in 1958, the year it was first published and the year I ran away from Phillips Exeter Academy and went looking for a revolution.

Since 1958, perhaps since 1058, the multifaceted, lush, Indian sort of Buddhism Kerouac preferred has returned to the planet from Tibet, after having been lost outside of Central Asia for a thousand years. Indian Universal Vehicle, Mahayana Buddhism and its monastic university institutions—vibrant communities of monks led by scientific sages, some of them adept explorers of inner universes, who accumulated mountains of texts in vast, multistoried "Libraries of Alexandria"—were destroyed by Islamized Persian and Turkic invasions and occupations of the Indian subcontinent, and its Great Mother of Civilizations was further obscured by Christianized European waves of invasion, domination, and exploitation.

I don't think I ever did read *On the Road* until just now for this assignment, and I don't think I would have liked the shuffling con man aspect of Dean Moriarty that much, though my own hitch-hikings and frenetic New York to California wanderings beginning in 1958 and running intermittently into 1961 were somewhat similar. I never managed to hop a freight, though, and I admire Kerouac for his knowledge and guts in doing that.

A question has apparently been hanging over Kerouac as to whether he really understood much about the Dharma, as if he were not really genuine in his understanding of enlightenment, or some such entity. Alan Watts was heard to say that he might have had "some Zen flesh but no Zen bones," referring to the title of a work by another writer on Zen, the redoubtable Paul Reps. And Gary Snyder, who spent years in Zen monasteries and is himself today a kind of Zen Roshi master as well as a poet, may have thought Kerouac didn't quite get it, though he remained a loving friend. There is no doubt that his tragic addiction to alcohol, which cut his life and practice short at a tender forty-seven years of age, is evidence that whatever enlightenment he had attained was short of perfect buddhahood, as buddhas don't usually drink themselves to premature death, since such doesn't help anyone else and that's all that buddhas do naturally. But who can really lay claim to that sort of transcendent physical and mental cosmic transmutation? In the vast psychological literature of the Buddhists, there are many analyses of the various stages of enlightenment; according to them it is quite possible to be enlightened to a certain degree and still prey to human failings. In fact, one becomes a *bodhisattva,* or hero for enlightenment, just by sincerely resolving and vowing to become perfectly enlightened in some future life, near or far, for the sake of developing the knowledge and ability to free all sensitive beings from suffering. That is, not all bodhisattvas are celestial or divine entities. Many are human, all too human.

The thing about Kerouac that might have made him less accepted among early California Buddhists—Gary Snyder and Alan Watts and others—was that he was not so taken by the Ch'an/Zen line of things, though he loved the writings of Han Shan, the "cold mountain" poetic meditations transmitted by Snyder. Kerouac was more moved by the Indian Mahayana line, which emerges both in the work at hand, the sweet "lake of light" story of the Buddha's life, and in his *Some of the Dharma* book notes composed for the benefit of his friend, dear Allen Ginsberg, which also gives us a record of Jack's own study.

Kerouac clearly loved the compassion stuff, what the Tibetans call the "magnificent deeds lineage" descended from Maitreya and Asanga. He loved dogs and they loved him. The Tibetans have a tradition, perhaps coming from the famous story of Asanga meeting Maitreya in the form of a dog, that the future Buddha Maitreya manifests generously in the form of dogs, ahead of his Buddha incarnation far in the future, in order to encourage depressed and frightened people to rise above their fears and develop trust and affection for another sentient being.

Significant is the note Kerouac gave Gary Snyder on the latter's departure for Japan and further years of Zen practice, as recorded in the semifictional *Dharma Bums;* "MAY YOU USE THE DIAMOND CUTTER OF MERCY." (Of course, as *Dharma Bums* is semifictional, you can't tell if he really gave him such a note or just wished he did; but the point is the same.) The Diamond Cutter is one of the *Prajnaparamita Sutras,* Transcendent Wisdom highest Mahayana sutras, and mercy and compassion were the facets of the wisdom of enlightenment that most spoke to Kerouac's Christo-Buddhist heart, which he didn't want Gary to lose sight of with his macho samurai focus on Zen. I love Kerouac's statement later in the novel, when he spends a summer in a fire-lookout cabin on Desolation Peak in Washington State's Skagit Range: "Whenever I heard thunder in the mountains it was like the iron of my mother's love."

He called the Buddha the "Jesus of Asia," even "sweeter than Jesus," and in *Wake Up* he relies extensively on Dwight Goddard's anthology *A Buddhist Bible* (Goddard, being a Christian, tended to emphasize aspects of Buddhism that resembled his own faith). At the beginning of *Wake Up*, Kerouac quotes Goddard's own dedication: "Adoration to Jesus Christ, the Messiah of the Christian World; Adoration to Gotama Sakyamuni, The Appearance-Body of the Buddha.—A BUDDHIST PRAYER in the Monastery of Santa Barbara, Written by Dwight Goddard." Kerouac here openly approves of adoring both "saviors" equally.

The Zen tradition developed in Japan in the context of a centuries' long taming of the samurai violence of the warriors of that nation, and so Kerouac's not having "Zen Bones" seems to be a reference precisely to his softness, his exaltation of kindness and gentleness, his love of dogs and their love of him. He also seemed less free-wheeling sexually than some of the other Beats, a bit shy and perhaps a bit more considerate of his women friends. He certainly was well loved, having been a legendary athlete as a youth, a truly handsome and elegant man, a celebrity writer lionized for a while in the 1950s and early 1960s. He would have been in his eighties today, and very much would have enjoyed the "rising sun of the Dharma" that is happening now in America, as prophetically promised to me one morning in 1964 by my old Mongolian spiritual friend, Geshe Wangyal, as we finished setting the big brass om mani padme hum prayer wheels on the porch of the Labsum Shedrub Ling (Lamaist Buddhist Monastery) building in Freewood Acres, New Jersey.

Kerouac was very much brought up a Catholic. His family was deeply Catholic and it seems they were suspicious of his romance with Buddha and Buddhism. His many critical interpreters seem to insist that he remained a Catholic, and he certainly did have a strong attachment to Jesus and Mother Mary. There is no doubt that he loved both Jesus and Buddha. Most scholars maintain that Kerouac was "really" a Christian through and through and his Buddhism some sort of side interest. Being a Protestant apostate myself, I have noted that our American cultured types are still uncomfortable about Buddhism, puzzled by it, and even artists heavily indebted to Buddhism or "the East" are reluctant to acknowledge that debt, until perhaps late in their careers.

In this context, we should consider why people tend to think that Kerouac's love for Jesus and spiritual (not the church variety so heavily compromised by dogma) Christianity implies that he did not understand and appreciate Buddhism (had he known better its various institutionalized forms he would no doubt have insisted on a non–church-dominated form of spiritual Buddhism). Do we need to reevaluate the relationship between Buddhism and Christianity?

Mahayana Buddhists are fond of embracing Christianity as fully resonant with their deepest intent. Christians often recoil from this embrace and emphasize their difference and, of course, their uniqueness. There is no doubt that the existence of an Absolute, Omnipotent yet Compassionate, Creator God is not believable to any educated Buddhist. That being said, relational, quite powerful, creative Gods are fully accepted and are an important part of the Buddha story, though they are not necessarily considered any more enlightened than most humans. The Gods of the many different heavenly levels and realms present in Buddhist cosmologies are immensely powerful and intelligent, very much absorbed in extremely long-lived, unimaginable rounds of lavish pleasure, and so are considered in danger of thinking that the egocentric life cycle is just fine and they really are the center of the universe—the very definition of the cosmic ignorance or misknowledge that is the root of the unremitting suffering of the unenlightened life.

But beyond this metaphysical difference about the status of God or the Gods, Mahayana Buddhism and Christianity arose and spread only one well-traveled ocean apart at the same time in Eurasian history. It was a time when stabilizing universal empires were spawning a new, more caring, more paternalistic form of imperial kingship, a time when divinity was being reenvisioned as balancing its terrible aspects with the loving concern for individuals so well represented by the celestial bodhisattva saviors such as Avalokiteshvara and Tara and messianic saviors such as Jesus and the Virgin Mary.

Jesus' life and main teachings, though embedded within the metaphysic and presented in the culture of a fearsome Omnipotent Creator, could have been that of an itinerant Buddhist "Great Adept" (Mahasiddha). His central message was the same as the Mahayana's: that divine love and compassion are the essential and most powerful energy of the universe. His provocation of oppressive rulers and challenge to them to do their utmost to put him to death was in fact precisely in order to show that they could not succeed in doing so, thus indicating the supremacy of the power of that love. He proved it to the satisfaction of his followers over thousands of years by showing his ability to overcome death and violence, proving that his love-body could rise up even from the cruelest crucifixion as a fountain of eternal life that lived luminously beyond any particular embodiment. The reincarnation teaching of "soul-transmigration" common in his time and culture (banned only two and a half centuries later by order of the emperor Constantine) made this kind of adept-like achievement plausible to his disciples and their successors, with a few exceptions.

There are many such stories of the Great Adepts of ancient India. The Buddha himself calmed by his mere gentle presence an enraged wild elephant sent to kill him by the patricidal king of Magadha. The young monk who converted the emperor Ashoka from being a paragon of cruelty to being a patron of the Noble Community (the Sangha, which Kerouac called the "Church") caught the emperor's attention by levitating suspended in a cool bubble of energy over the raging flames of a cauldron of boiling oil. The enlightened alchemist Nagarjuna possessed the secret of immortality and lived six hundred years. The adept Naropa was burned at the stake with his female consort and both remained unharmed in the midst of the flames. India was rife with tales (modern folks will think "legends," which is fine) of holy sages who demonstrated love's power over death.

Then there are the teachings: Jesus' beatitudes, his extraordinary teachings on nonviolence, to turn the other cheek to your enemy's blows, to give your cloak when your shirt is demanded of you, to go beyond loving your friends and relatives and learn to love your enemy, and the central injunction to love your neighbor as yourself. These teachings are totally consonant with the Buddhist ethic of nonviolence, and resonate powerfully with the Mahayana's messianic emphasis on selflessness, heroic tolerance, love, and compassion. On the wisdom level, Jesus' statements that the kingdom of God lies within you are fully compatible with the Buddhist vision of the Buddha-nature in all beings, or Nagarjuna's famous statement of nonduality, that the deepest reality is ultimate voidness as the womb of relational compassion (*shunyatakarunagarbham*). And Jesus' powerful statement to the legalist priestly hierarchy he faced that "I am the way, the light, and the truth!" can be understood not as dictating religious exclusivism for a particular church or faith and furious intolerance of others, but rather as insisting by living example that divinity and salvation for each person lies within herself or himself as an individual, and not through membership in some denomination or institution.

The deeds of St. Thomas in the Kerala area of India are very much like those of any Buddhist itinerant monk and preacher. The Nicene Council's editing of the Gospels, especially the excision of St. Thomas's Gospel, among others; the banning of the Buddhist or Indian doctrine of transmigration of souls, such as was championed even by the semi-martyred Origen; and Constantine's transformation of Buddhism into a tool of the Roman state—these obscure the Christ-Buddha connection; but, nevertheless, it was perceived by Mani and others closer to the time. Professor Thomas McEvilley mentions "early 3rd–4th century Christian writers such as Hippolytus and Epiphanius" who wrote about a man named Scythianus, who brought to Alexandria "the doctrine of the Two Principles" from India around 50 A.D. According to them, Scythianus' pupil Terebinthus presented himself as a "Buddha" and went to Palestine and Judaea, where he met the Apostles, who apparently condemned him. He then settled in Babylon, where he transmitted his teachings

to Mani, who himself founded what could be called Persian syn-
cretic Buddho-Christianity, known as Manicheism, which was the
youthful religion of Augustine of Hippo, who later condemned it.

So in spite of the insistence by Christians that their teachings
are sui generis and come down only from God and have no connection with any other movement on the planet, Mahayana Buddhism
and Christianity have very strong "family resemblances." It is likely
that Kerouac understood the deeper, broader dimensions of Mahayana Buddhism better than his peers, either those like myself,
who were strongly motivated to break away from their Christian
background, or those who were receiving their knowledge through
the prism of East Asian Chinese and Japanese cultures, and especially through the Ch'an/Zen connection, where meditation and
samurai-like hardball "no-thought" are emphasized.

Most important to examine is Kerouac's personal understanding
of enlightenment, which he seems to assume is the experience of the
oneness of all things, and yet he allows also for the persistence of
engagement with a transformed relativity. Though he oftens mentions
no-thing-ness and even nothing, he refuses to reify any sort of disappearance, and most often talks of "the holy emptiness," not nothingness, and emphasizes that "emptiness is form" just as much as "form
is emptiness." He blew me away by referring to the "Womb of the
Tathagata," and seems comfortable in the profound realm that Nagarjuna calls *shunyatakarunagarbham*, "emptiness the womb of compassion." He offers many accounts of his personal experiences in
meditation (he knows all the original terms, *dhyana, samadhi, samapatti*)
toward the end of *Some of the Dharma*. But the following passage from
The Dharma Bums might be the one he would prefer I quote:

What did I care about the squawk of the little very self which wanders everywhere? I was dealing in outblownness, cut-off-ness, snipped, blownoutness, putoutness, turned-off-ness, nothing-happens-ness, gone-ness, gone-out-ness, the snapped link, nir, link, vana, snap! "The dust of my thoughts collected into a globe," I thought, "in this ageless solitude," I thought, and really smiled, because I was seeing the white light everywhere everything at last.

The warm wind made the pines talk deep one night when I began to experience what is called "Samapatti," which in Sanskrit means Transcendental Visits. I'd got a little drowsy in the mind but was somehow physically wide awake sitting erect under my tree when suddenly I saw flowers, pink worlds of walls of them, salmon pink, in the *Shh* of silent woods (obtaining nirvana is like locating silence) and I saw an ancient vision of Dipankara Buddha who was the Buddha who never said anything. Dipankara as a vast snowy Pyramid Buddha with bushy wild black eyebrows like John L. Lewis and a terrible stare, all in an old location, an ancient snowy field like Alban ("A *new* field!" had yelled the Negro preacherwoman), the whole vision making my hair rise. I remember the strange magic final cry that it evoked in me, whatever it means: *Colyalcolor*. It, the vision, was devoid of any sensation of I being myself, it was pure egolessness, just simply wild ethereal activities devoid of any wrong predicates . . . devoid of effort, devoid of mistake. "Everything's all right," I thought. "Form is emptiness and emptiness is form and we're here forever in one form or another which is empty. What the dead have accomplished, this rich silent hush of the Pure Awakened Land."

I felt like crying out over the woods and rooftops of North Carolina announcing the glorious and simple truth. Then I said "I've got my full rucksack pack and it's spring. I'm going to go southwest to the dry land, to the long lone land of Texas and Chihuahua and the gay streets of Mexico night, music coming out of doors, girls, wine, weed, wild hats, viva! What does it matter! Like the ants that have nothing to do but dig all day, I have nothing to do but do what I want and be kind and remain nevertheless uninfluenced by imaginary judgments and pray for the light." Sitting in my Buddha-arbor, therefore, in that "colyalcolor" wall of flowers pink and red and ivory white, among aviaries of magic transcendent birds recognizing my awakening mind with sweet weird cries (the pathless lark), in the ethereal perfume, mysteriously ancient, the bliss of the Buddha-fields, I saw that my life was a vast glowing empty page and I could do anything I wanted.

"Colyalcolor" is a mystery for sure—it reminds me of *Kooroo-koolleh*, the name of the ruby-red goddess bodhisattva who is the archetype of passionate compassion. She stands in a dancing pose, stark naked except for garlands of flowers, and holds a flower bow with bee string, shooting flower arrows to open beings' hearts. But I'm not saying that was what Jack's amazing word really meant. Perhaps it is the name of the "Buddha-field" he will create when he perfects his "awakener-ship" someday. D. T. Suzuki was funny. When Jack reportedly asked him upon meeting if he could stay with him forever, he answered, "Sometime." You can always get a sense of how someone really feels by how they explain the Buddha's enlightenment and basic teachings. The only discordant note in his experience is "I have nothing to do but do what I want," which evinces a trace of the "nothing matters after all" sort of nihilistic misunderstanding of emptiness and perhaps the kernel of his inability to take his alcoholism seriously enough to get free of it and preserve himself and his genius for our benefit somewhat longer than 1969. Fortunately, Kerouac goes on to say, "and be kind and nevertheless remain uninfluenced by imaginary judgments and pray for the light," which evinces his deeper instinct that the nonduality of voidness and form, nirvana and samsara, mandates that the free person remain causally committed to the improvement of the conditions of others in the illusory unreal relative world.

Wake Up Itself

What a thrill to read *Wake Up,* Kerouac's vision of the life of Shakyamuni, the supreme Buddha emanation of our age! The long, streaming style makes the book majestic and something that you absorb in one sitting, like a symphony, culminating in a way in the *Shurangama Sutra's* heroic march vision of the world dissolving in the diamond samadhi, and seeing the Tathagata Buddha ("Thus-gone Awakened One") floating in the flower-petal universe beyond the body and the system there of seven elements: earth, water, fire, wind, space, perception, consciousness. *Wake Up* has a basic flavor of nonduality in that section but then returns to the more conventional dualist Buddhist vision at the time of the parinirvana ("final nirvana"), treating it as a dreamless sleep of extinction, since Kerouac did not have available to him the exquisite paradox of the Buddha's revelation of his eternal presence at the moment of his final disappearance as a distinct body, as revealed in the Lotus and *Mahaparinirvana Sutras.*

Wake Up was written during the first half of 1955. In January of that year, Kerouac had moved with his mother from Richmond Hill, New York, into the house of his sister Nin, who lived in Rocky Mount, North Carolina. Away from the hectic life of New York City, Kerouac was able to immerse himself in the idea of leading an ascetic life in the tradition of the Buddha—he sat by himself for hours, meditating under the clear night stars. The title page of the finished manuscript reads "Wake Up Prepared by Jack Kerouac," but this had not always been the book's title. Originally called "Your Essential Mind: The Story of the Buddha," Kerouac also referred to it at various times as "my Buddhist handbook," "Buddha Tells Us," and "Buddhahood: The Essence of Reality."

Kerouac does not attempt to hide his copious use of his sources, remarking at the beginning in his Author's Note: "There is no way to separate and name the countless sources that have poured into this lake of light. . . . The heart of the book is an embellished précis of the mighty Surangama Sutra." (The first "s" of the title should be written "sh" to be phonetically accurate without a diacritic mark.) "I have designed this to be a handbook for Western understanding of the ancient Law." (He uses the old translators' use of "law" for "Dharma," which is not wrong in general, but is inaccurate in this context; it should be "truth" or "teaching.") "The purpose is to convert." (Here Kerouac surely does not mean to enroll people in any formal Buddhist denomination, but rather to convert them to the heart's purpose in life, to the grand wisdom vision of the divinity within, and of the natural love and kindness in relationships.)

Kerouac also draws heavily on the Pali sources about the Buddha's life, orally ancient but not written down until the fifth century C.E., and from the second century C.E. biographical poem *Buddhacharita,* by the great Asvhaghosha. He tends to mix up some of the details of most versions of the Buddha's life, conventionally dated at 563–482 B.C.E. (though Tibetans date him in the ninth century B.C.E., and recent European scholars move him up into the fourth century B.C.E.). I will not concern myself with such details but will simply highlight some things in the text I find particularly beautiful.

Early in the book, Kerouac says, "Buddha means the awakened one. Until recently most people thought of Buddha as a big fat rococo sitting figure with his belly out, laughing, as represented in millions of tourist trinkets and dime store statuettes here in the western world. . . . This man was no slob-like figure of mirth, but a serious and tragic prophet, the Jesus Christ of India and almost all Asia. The followers of the religion he founded, Buddhism, the religion of the Great Awakening from the dream of existence, number in the hundreds of millions today." I'm not sure why Kerouac thought Buddha was "tragic" rather than triumphant, as indeed he seemed to feel in the vision he recounts above in *The Dharma Bums.* Maybe because of the Buddha's first noble truth, that "unenlightened life is bound to be frustrating, and so all suffering." When Kerouac says Buddha was "the Jesus Christ of India and almost all Asia," he repeats his apostasy from orthodox Catholicism, by putting the two on the same level.

A few pages later, Kerouac shows his awareness of the "four formless realms" and the fact that they are none of them nirvana: "Alara Kalama [Siddhartha, the young Buddha's first ascetic teacher] expounded the teaching called 'the realm of nothingness,' and prac-

ticed self-mortification to prove that he was free from his body."
This is especially significant, since almost all translators and scholars in the 1950s thought that "emptiness" and "nothingness" were
the same thing, and so spread the misconception that Buddhists
were ultimately nihilistic. Kerouac shows precisely here his knowledge of the difference.

Kerouac evinces his realistic view and presages his eventual "samapatti," by explaining accurately how Siddhartha critiqued the
"oversoul" (*Paramatma*) theory of the Brahmins: "Of Arada Udarama
[his other ascetic teacher at this time] he asked: 'With respect to
old age, disease, and death, how are these things to be escaped?'
The hermit replied that by the 'I' being rendered pure, forthwith
there was true deliverance. This was the ancient teaching propounding the Immortal Soul, the 'Purusha,' Atman, the Oversoul that
went from life to life getting more and more or less and less pure,
with its final goal pure soulhood in heaven. But the holy intelligence
of Gotama perceived that this 'Purusha' was no better than a ball
being bounced around according to concomitant circumstances,
whether in heaven, hell, or on earth, and as long as one held this
view there was no perfect escape from birth and destruction of
birth. The birth of anything means death of the thing: and this is
decay, this is horror, change, this is pain."

Kerouac goes on to recount, anticipating his later vision,
"Approaching now his moment of . . . compassion the young Saint
saw all things, men sitting in groves, trees, sky, different views
about the soul, different selves, as one unified emptiness in the
air, one imaginary flower, the significance of which was unity and
undividable-ness, all of the same dreamstuff, universal and secretly

pure." Here he expresses the Mahayana nonduality, though he is still using Theravada sources: "He saw that existence was like the light of a candle: the light of the candle and the extinction of the light of the candle were the same thing. . . . Gotama saw the peace of the Buddha's Nirvana. Nirvana means blown out, as of a candle. But because the Buddha's Nirvana is beyond existence, and conceives neither the existence or non-existence of the light of a candle, or an immortal soul, or any <u>thing</u>, it is not even Nirvana, it is neither the light of the candle known as Sangsara (this world) nor the blown-out extinction of the light of the candle known as Nirvana (the no-world) but awake beyond these arbitrarily established conceptions." I am awed and amazed at Kerouac's elucidation of profound nonduality in this context.

The description of the Buddha's enlightenment in *Wake Up* is especially moving, very majestic and insightful. It is too long to quote here in its entirety. Kerouac alternates between quoting Pali sources and his own "embellishments." I will pick out a few choice passages.

> The blessed hermit went to Budhgaya. At once the ancient dream of the Buddhas of Old possessed him as he gazed at the noble groves of palm and mango and <u>ficus religiosa</u> fig trees; in the rippling afternoon he passed beneath their branches, lonely and bemused, yet with a stirring of premonition in his heart that something great was about to happen here . . . rediscovering the lost and ancient path of the Tathagata (He of Suchnesshood); re-unfolding the primal dew drop of the world; like the swan of pity descending in the lotus pool, and settling, great joy overwhelmed him at the sight of the tree which he

chose to sit under as per agreement with all the Buddha-lands and assembled Buddha-things which are No-things in the emptiness of sparkling intuition all around like swarms of angels and Bodhisattvas in mothlike density radiating endlessly towards the center of the void in ADORATION. "Everywhere is Here," intuited the saint. . . . "I WILL NOT RISE FROM THIS SPOT," he resolved within himself, "UNTIL, FREED FROM CLINGING, MY MIND ATTAINS TO DELIVERANCE FROM ALL SORROW."

Many words have been written about this holy moment in the now famous spot beneath this Bodhi-Tree, or Wisdom-Tree. It was not an agony in the garden, it was a bliss beneath the tree. (Here is Kerouac's comparison with Christ.) It was not the resurrection of anything, but the annihilation of all things. (He slips into the relative-absolute dualism of Theravada.) What came to Buddha in those hours was the realization that all things come from a cause and go to dissolution, and therefore all things are impermanent, all things are unhappy, and thereby and most mysterious, all things are unreal. (Here is Kerouac's apprehension of the essential Buddhist insight into causation; he comes later to the famous verse, the key mantra of all Buddhism.)

By nightfall he reposed peaceful and quiet. He entered into deep and subtle contemplation. Every kind of holy ecstasy in order passed before his eyes. During the first watch of the night he entered on "right perception" and in recollection all former births passed before his eyes. . . . Knowing full well that the essence of existence is of onesuchness, what birth could not his Bright, Mysterious, Intuitive

Essence of Mind recall? As though he had been all things, and only because there had never been a true "he," but all things, and so all things were the same thing, and it was within the purview of the Universal Mind, which was the Only Mind past, present, and future. . . . It had been a long time already finished, the ancient dream of life, the tears of the many-mothered sadness, the myriads of fathers in the dust, eternities of lost afternoons of sisters and brothers, the sleepy cock crow, the insect cave, the pitiful instinct all wasted on emptiness, the great huge drowsy Golden Age sensation that opened in his brain that this knowledge was older than the world. . . . In the ears of the Buddha as he thus sat in brilliant and sparkling craft of intuition, so that light like Transcendental Milk dazzled in the invisible dimness of his closed eyelids, was heard the unvarying pure hush of the sighing sea of hearing, seething, receding, as he more or less recalled the consciousness of the sound, though in itself it was always the same steady sound, only his consciousness of it varied and receded, like low tide flats and the salty water sizzling and sinking in the sand, the sound neither outside nor within the ear but everywhere, the pure sea of hearing, the Transcendental Sound of Nirvana heard by children in cribs and on the moon and in the heart of howling storms, and in which the young Buddha now heard a teaching going on, a ceaseless instruction wise and clear from all the Buddhas of Old that had come before him and all the Buddhas a-Coming. Beneath the distant cricket howl occasional noises like the involuntary peep of sleeping dream birds, or scutters of little fieldmice, or a vast breeze in the trees disturbed the peace of this Hearing but the noises were merely accidental, the Hearing received all noises and accidents in its sea but remained as ever undisturbed, truly unpenetrated, and neither replenished nor diminished, as self-pure as empty space. Under the blazing stars the King of the Law, enveloped in the divine tranquillity of this Transcendental Sound of the Diamond Ecstasy, rested moveless.

Then in the middle watch of night, he reached to knowledge of the pure Angels, and beheld before him every creature, as one sees images upon a mirror; all creatures born and born again to die, noble and mean, the poor and rich, reaping the fruit of right or evil doing, and sharing happiness or misery in consequence. . . . The groundmist of 3 A.M. rose with all the dolors of the world. . . . Birth of bodies is the direct cause of death of bodies. Just as, implantation of its seed was the cause of the cast off rose.

Then looking further, Where does birth come from? he saw it came from life-deeds done elsewhere; then scanning those deeds, he saw they were not framed by a creator, not self caused, nor personal existences nor were they either uncaused; he saw they themselves obtained along a further chain of causes, cause upon cause, concatenative links joining the fetters binding all that is form— poor form, mere dust and pain.

Then, as one who breaks the first bamboo joint finds all the rest easy to separate, having discerned the cause of death as birth, and the cause of birth as deeds, he gradually came to see the truth; death comes from birth, birth comes from deeds, deeds come from attachment, attachment comes from desire, desire comes from perception, perception comes from sensation, sensation comes from the six sense organs, the six sense organs come from individuality, individuality comes from consciousness. [Here Kerouac heads off through the all-important twelve links of dependent origination.] . . .

In him, thus freed, arose knowledge and freedom, and he knew that rebirth was at an end, and that the goal had been reached.

Kerouac goes on to list the four noble truths and the eightfold path. Then he opens up a more Mahayana vision:

And he knew as he sat there lustrous with all wisdom, perfect in gifts, that the way of perfect knowledge had been handed down to him from Buddhas Innumerable of Old that had come before in all ten directions of all ten quarters of the universe where he now saw them in a mighty vision assembled in brightness and power sitting on their intrinsic thrones in the Glorious Lotus Blossoms everywhere throughout phenomena and space and forever giving response to the needs of all sentient life in all the kingdoms of existence, past, present, and future.

With the discernment of the grand truths and their realization in life the Rishi became enlightened; he thus attained <u>Sambodhi</u> (Perfect Wisdom) and became a Buddha. Rightly has Sambodhi been called, it can be accomplished only by self help without the extraneous aid of a teacher or a god. . . . The morning sunbeams brightened with the dawn, the dustlike mist dispersing, disappeared. The moon and stars paled their faint light, the barriers of the night were all removed. He had finished this the first great lesson and the final lesson and the lesson of old; entering the great Rishi's house of Dreamless Sleep, fixed in holy trance, he had reached the source of exhaustless truth, the happiness that never ends and that had no beginning but was always already there within the True Mind.

Not by anxious use of outward means, had Buddha unveiled the

True Mind and ended suffering, but by resting quietly in thoughtful silence. This is the supreme fact of blessed rest.

He was <u>sihibhuto</u>, cooled.

About one quarter into the book, Kerouac describes the triumph of Buddha as world-teacher:

Thus Tathagata, He-Who-Has-Attained-to-Suchness-of-Mind and sees no more differentiation of various creatures and phenomena, who entertains no more definite conceptions of self, other selves, many divided selves, or one undivided universal self, to whom the world is no longer noticeable, except as a pitiful apparition, yet without arbitrary conception either of its existence or non-existence, as one thinks not to measure the substantiality of a dream but only to wake from it; thus Tathagata, piously composed and silent, radiant with glory, shedding light around, rose from under his Tree of Enlightenment, and with unmatched dignity advanced alone over the dreamlike earth as if surrounded by a crowd of followers, thinking, "To fulfill my ancient oath, to rescue all not yet delivered, I will follow out my ancient vow. Let those that have ears to hear master the noble path of salvation."

A few pages later, we get a hint of where Kerouac gets his title: "For to these ancient monks, clearly perceiving birth as the cause of death, and deeds of lust as the cause of birth, the Buddha was like one standing on the bank calling to the worldly man drifting down the current 'Ho there! Wake up! the river in your dream may seem pleasant, but below it is a lake with rapids and crocodiles, the river is evil desire, the lake is the sensual life, its waves are anger, its rapids are lust, and the crocodiles are the women-folk.' "

Kerouac homes in on the key mantra, in the words of the disciple Ashvajit: "Whatever things proceed from a cause, of them the Buddha has stated the cause and what their dissolution is. This is what the Great One teaches." *Om ye dharmah hetusvabhavah hetun tesham tathagata hi avadat tesham cha yo nirodho evam vadi mahashramanah.*

Kerouac also touches on the eventual happiness of the Buddha's father Suddhodana, and here I can imagine his fantasy of reconciliation with his own father, Leo, which never really happened, as I understand from scholars: "Having heard from his son how to cast off fear and escape the evil ways of birth, and in a manner of such dignity and tenderness, the King himself left his kingly estate and country and entered on the calm flowings of thoughts, the gate of the true law of eternality. Sweet in meditation, dew Suddhodana drank. In the night, recalling his son with pride, he looked up at the infinite stars and suddenly realized 'How glad I am to be alive to reverence this starry universe!' then 'But it's not a case of being alive and the starry universe is not necessarily the starry universe' and he realized the utter strangeness and yet commonness of the unsurpass-able wisdom of the Buddha."

A third of the way through *Wake Up*, Kerouac describes the Buddha as the supreme "Dharma bum," in an unbelievably brilliant passage I feel compelled to repeat:

> Buddha accepted food both good or bad, whatever came, from rich
> or poor, without distinction, and having filled his alms-dish, he then

returned back to the solitude, where he meditated his prayer for the emancipation of the world from its bestial grief and incessant bloody deeds of death and birth, death and birth, the ignorant gnashing screaming wars, the murder of dogs, the histories, follies, parent beating child, child tormenting child, lover ruining lover, robber raiding niggard, leering, cocky, crazy, wild, blood-louts moaning for more blood-lust, utter sots, running up and down simpleminded among charnels of their own making, simpering everywhere, mere <u>tsorises</u> and dream-pops, one monstrous beast raining forms from a central glut, all buried in unfathomable darkness crowing for rosy hope that can only be complete extinction, at base innocent and without any vestige of self-nature whatever; for should the causes and conditions of the ignorant insanity of the world be removed, the nature of its non-insane non-ignorance would be revealed, like the child of dawn entering heaven through the morning in the lake of the mind, the Pure, True Mind, the source, Original Perfect Essence, the empty void radiance, divine by nature, the sole reality, Immaculate, Universal, Eternal, One Hundred Percent Mental, upon which all this dream-filled darkness is imprinted, upon which these unreal bodying forms appear for what seems to be a moment and then disappear for what seems to be eternity.

Halfway through the book, Kerouac recites his refrain: "All is empty everywhere forever, wake up! The mind is fool and limited, to take these senses, petty thwartings in a dream, as reality; as if the deeps of the ocean were moved by the wind that ripples the waves. And that wind is ignorance." And further on, "Everything is taking place in your mind, like a dream. As soon as you wake up and stop dreaming, your mind returns to its original emptiness and purity. In truth, your mind has already returned to its original emptiness and purity, and this world is but a limping shadow. Why do you still so easily forget this natural, wonderful, and enlightened Mind of perfect Purity—this mysterious Mind of radiant Brightness?" (This seems a mix of quotes from the *Shurangama Sutra*.)

Then he gets down to the real heart of the *Sutra*:

> "Look carefully! Stare through the sight of things and you will only see the Great Heart of Compassion of all the Buddhas of Old beyond belief. This is <u>Yathabhutam</u>, the seeing of things truly. . . . However, people of the world, spectral giants inside mind, being ignorant of the principle that governs their own existence, become bewildered in the entanglements of causes and conditions and naturalism, they think the earth carries signs of an inherent self-nature of its own and call it 'nat-ural' and 'Mother Nature' with all the mental trees independent of their own bodies, they think that it exists due to causes such as creation by some self-created and self-remembering Creator Self who made them after his own image and that their existence comes under the conditions of 'time,' atoms, seasons, celestial interventions, personal destiny, all of which are wholly the discriminations of their mental consciousness and are merely figurative words having no meaning in reality."

(So much for Kerouac's supposed unaltered belief in the theo-logical dogmas of Creation.)

> "Ananda, naturally, you have never known that within your Womb of Tathagata the essential nature of Consciousness is enlight-

ening and intelligent, that is, for instance, it neither is conscious of perception of sight of spring and pools, nor not-conscious, it is conscious of the Dharma of No-Things. Ananda, are you going to say that that rock and that pool are two different things? It were better if you were to say that each one is a Buddha, and that we only need one Buddha because all things are No-Things, and that all things are therefore Buddhas. This is the Diamond Knowledge, all the rest is knowledge about ripples and balloons. This enlightened intuition is your true Essence of Consciousness and it is like the intrinsic nature of space."

Thereupon Ananda and all the assembly, having received this wonderful and profound instruction from the Lord Tathagata and having attained to a state of perfect accommodation of mind and perfect emancipation of mind from all remembrances, thinking and desires, became perfectly free in both body and mind. Each one of them understood clearly that the mind can reach to all the ten quarters of the universes and that their perception of sight can reach to all the ten quarters also. It was just as clear to them as though it was a blade of grass held in their hand. They saw that all the worldly phenomena was nothing but their own wonderful, intelligent, original Mind of Enlightenment, their physical bodies begotten from their parents seemed like specks of dust blowing about in the open space of the ten quarters of the universes. Who would notice their existence? Their physical body was like a speck of foam floating about on a vast and trackless ocean, with nothing distinctive about it to indicate from whence it came, and if it disappeared whither it went. They realized very clearly, that they, at last, had acquired their own wonderful Mind, a Mind that was Permanent and Indestructible.

Further on, when we compare the description of Ananda's enlightenment in the *Shurangama* with Kerouac's description in *The Dharma Bums*, we see why he said his long quotes from the *Sutra* were the heart of the biography:

> Suddenly it seemed that all the trees of the Jeta Park, and all the waves lapping on the shores of its lakes, were singing the music of the Dharma, and all the intersecting rays of brightness were like a net of splendor set with jewels and over arching them all. Such a marvelous sight had never been imagined by the assembled holy devotees and held them all in silence and awe. Unwittingly they passed into the blissful peace of the Diamond Samadhi, that is, every one immediately listened to the intense and mysterious roar of silence, the entire multitude of twelve hundred and thirty three, and upon them all there seemed to fall like a gentle rain the soft petals of many different colored lotus blossoms—blue and crimson, yellow and white—all blending together and being reflected into the open space of heaven in all the tints of the spectrum. Moreover, all the differentiations of mountains in their minds, and seas and rivers and forests of the Saha-suffering world blended into one another and faded away leaving only the flower-adorned unity of the Primal Cosmos. In the center of it all, seated on pure lotus, they saw the Tathagata, Already-Thus, the Pearl and the Pillar of the world.

The point in the *Sutra* where Manjusri exhorts Ananda in the inward-turning contemplative practice may very well underly Kerouac's purported method of direct stream-of-consciousness writing, which he may be considering to be the nondiscriminating mind flowing with the nondual emptiness forms of the world.

> "Ananda, should reverse your outward perception of hearing and listen inwardly for the perfectly unified and intrinsic sound of your own Mind-Essence, for as soon as you have attained perfect accommodation, you will have attained to Supreme Enlightenment.
>
> "This is the only way to Nirvana, and it has been followed by all the Tathagatas of the past. Moreover, it is for all the Bodhisattva-Mahasattvas of the present and for all in the future if they are to hope for Perfect Enlightenment. Not only did Avaloki-Tesvara attain Perfect Enlightenment in long ages past by this Golden Way, but in the present, I also, am one of them . . . but for laymen, this common method of concentrating the mind on its sense of hearing, turning it inward by this Door of Dharma to hear the Transcendental Sound of his Essential Mind, is most feasible and wise."

A few pages on, Kerouac sets forth an ethic he clearly aspired to follow himself: "The Four Precepts are: 1. Wake up, cease sexual lust, sexual lust leads to multiplicity and strife and suffering. 2. Wake up, cease the tendency to unkindness toward others, unkindness is the murderer of the life of wisdom. 3. Wake up, cease greediness and stealing, you should look upon your own body as not being your own but as being one with the bodies of all other sentient beings. 4. Wake up, cease secret insincerity and lying, there should be no falsehood in your life, there is no hiding anything in a shattering dewdrop."

Here, Kerouac marks an interesting resonance with Jesus: "Elated and believing, perceiving the serenity, the moral earnestness, the sweet reasonableness of the Master, more and more disciples joined the Brotherhood. Of his Twelve Great Disciples, 500 years before Christ and His Twelve, the Blessed One said: 'Save in my religion the Twelve Great Disciples, who, being good themselves, rouse up the world and deliver it from indifference, are not to be found.'"

Near the end of the book, Kerouac introduces the final nirvana, with the Buddha consoling the distraught Ananda: "If things around us could be kept for aye, and were not liable to change or separation, then this would be salvation! Where can this be sought? That which you may all attain I have already told you, and tell you, to the end. There is love at the center of all things and all things are the same thing. Svaha! I am resolved, I look for rest. The one thing needful has been done, and has long been done."

He concludes with an insightful description of the Buddha's departure from his manifest embodiment into parinirvana, not, he notices, from the ninth contemplative state is if it were an annihilation beyond annihilation, but from the fourth state, on the event horizon boundary of the realm of infinite space, where mass becomes infinite at the speed of light:

> [H]e went successively through all the nine Dhyanas [contemplative states] in a direct order; then inversely he returned throughout and entered on the first, and then from the first he raised himself and entered on the Fourth Dhyana, the Dhyana of Neither Joy nor Suffer-

ing, utterly pure and equal, the original and eternal perfect essence of Mind. Leaving the state of Samadhi ecstasy, his soul without a resting-place forthwith he reached Pari-Nirvana, complete extinction of the form after it has died. . . . Voluntarily enduring infinite trials through numberless ages and births, that he might deliver mankind and all life, foregoing the right to enter Nirvana and casting himself again and again into Sangsara's stream of life and destiny for the sole purpose of teaching the way of liberation from sorrow and suffering, this is Buddha, who is everyone and everything, Aremideia the Light of the World, the Tathagata, Maitreya, the Coming Hero, the Walker of the terrace of earth, the Sitter under Trees, persistent, energetic, intensely human, the Great Wise Being of Pity and Tenderness.

The noble and superlative law of Buddha ought to receive the adoration of the world."

I have no idea who "Aremideia" is, possibly a version of Amitabha, Amitofo in Chinese, Amida in Japanese, the Buddha of Infinite Light and Infinite Life who maintains and resides in the Sukhavati paradise universe in the western direction beyond as many universes as there are grains of sand in sixty-two Ganges riverbeds. In any event, it's clear that Kerouac did live up to the charge given him in a vision granted by Avalokitesvara, the thousand-armed, thousand-eyed, eleven-headed bodhisattva of universal compassion, as reported in *The Dharma Bums*:

One night in a meditation vision Avalokitesvara the Hearer and Answerer of Prayer said to me "You are empowered to remind people

that they are utterly free" so I laid my hand on myself to remind myself first and then felt gay, yelled "Ta," opened my eyes, and a shooting star shot.

Robert A. F. Thurman

Jey Tsong Khapa Professor of
Indo-Tibetan Buddhist Studies, Columbia University

Woodstock, New York

June 18, 2008

WAKE UP

"Adoration to Jesus Christ,
the Messiah of the Christian World;
Adoration to Gotama Sakyamuni
The Appearance-Body of the Buddha."

—A BUDDHIST PRAYER in the
Monastery of Santa Barbara,
Written by Dwight Goddard

AUTHOR'S NOTE

This book follows what the Sutras say. It contains quotations from the Sacred Scriptures of the Buddhist Canon, some quoted directly, some mingled with new words, some not quotations but made up of new words of my own selection. The story line follows Gotama Buddha's life as represented in Asvhaghosha's "Buddha–Charita" and in Narasu's "Life of the Historic Buddha" with adornments and re-arrangements. There is no way to separate and name the countless sources that have poured into this lake of light, such as the Lankavatara Scripture, the Dhammapada, the Anguttara Nikaya, the Itivuttaka, the Digga Nikaya, the Majjhima Nikaya, the Theragatha, the Vinaya Pitaka, the Prajna-Paramita-Hridaya Sutra, the Samyutta Nikaya, even Chuangtse, Tao Teh King, the Life of Milarepa, the Mahayana Samgraha and a thousand places. The heart of the book is an embellished précis of the mighty Surangama Sutra whose author, who seems to be the greatest writer who ever lived, is unknown. He lived in the First Century A.D. and drew from the sources of his own time and wrote for the sake of Brightest Divine Enlightenment. I have designed this to be a handbook for Western understanding of the ancient Law. The purpose is to convert. May I live up to these words:- "To sing the praises of the lordly monk, and declare his acts from first to last, without self seeking and self honor, without desire for personal renown, but following what the scriptures say, to benefit the world, has been my aim." ASVHAGHOSHA, First Century A.D.

Buddha means the awakened one.

Until recently most people thought of Buddha as a big fat rococo sitting figure with his belly out, laughing, as represented in millions of tourist trinkets and dime store statuettes here in the western world. People didn't know that the actual Buddha was a handsome young prince who suddenly began brooding in his father's palace, staring through the dancing girls as though they weren't there, at the age of 29, till finally and emphatically he threw up his hands and rode out to the forest on his war horse and cut off his long golden hair with his sword and sat down with the holy men of the India of his day and died at the age of 80 a lean venerable wanderer of ancient roads and elephant woods. This man was no slob-like figure of mirth, but a serious and tragic prophet, the Jesus Christ of India and almost all Asia.

The followers of the religion he founded, Buddhism, the religion of the Great Awakening from the dream of existence, number in the hundreds of millions today. Few people in America and the West realized the extent and the profundity of religious establishment in the Orient. Few people knew that

Korea, Burma, Siam, Thibet, Japan and Pre-Red China are predominantly Buddhist countries as the United States, England, France, Italy, Mexico may be said to be predominantly Christian countries.

This young man who couldn't be tempted by a harem-full of beautiful girls because of the wisdom of his great sorrow, was Gotama, born Siddartha in 563 B.C., Prince of the Sakya Clan in the Gorakpur district of India. His mother, whose name, curiously, was "Maya," which in Sanskrit means "magic," died giving him birth. He was raised by his aunt Prajapati Gotami. As a youth he was a great athlete and horseman, as befits a member of the Kshatriya, the Warrior Caste. Legend tells of a sensational contest in which he bested all the other princes for the hand of Yasodhara.

He was married at sixteen to the Princess Yasodhara who bore him a son Rahula. His father the Maharajah Suddhodhana doted on him and plotted with his ministers to figure out ways to please him and take his mind off the deep sadness that grew and grew as he neared thirty. One day, riding through the royal gardens in the chariot, the Prince beheld an old man tottering in the road. "What kind of man is this? His head white and his shoulders bent, his eyes bleared and his body withered, holding a stick to support him along the way. Is his body suddenly dried up by the heat, or has he been born in this way? . . . Quickly turn your chariot and go back. Ever thinking on this subject of old age approaching, what pleasures now can these gardens afford, the years of my life like the fast-flying wind; turn your chariot and with speedy wheels take me to my palace." Then on seeing a dead man being borne to his bier nearby. "The followers are overwhelmed with grief, tearing their hair and wailing piteously . . . Is this the only dead man, or does the world contain like instances? O worldly men!" cried the unhappy young prince. "Beholding everywhere the body brought to dust, yet everywhere the more carelessly living; the heart is neither lifeless wood nor stone, and yet it thinks not ALL IS VANISHING . . ."

That night, on orders from the King who'd heard of this, Udayi the King's Minister commanded the girls to entice Prince Siddartha with their charms. They made many winsome moves, dropped casual shoulder silks, snaked their arms, arched their eyes, danced suggestively, caressed his wrists, some even pretended to be blushingly confused and removed roses from their bosoms crying "Oh is this yours or mine, youthful prince?" but in his mindfulness of woe the Prince was unmoved. At midnight the girls were all exhausted and asleep on various divans and pillows. Only the Prince was awake. "It is not that I am careless about beauty," he spoke to the dark, questioning Minister, "or am ignorant of the power of human joys, but only that I see on all the impress of change; therefore my heart is sad and heavy;

if these things were sure of lasting, without the ills of age, disease and death, then would I too take my fill of love; and to the end find no disgust or sadness. If you will undertake to cause these women's beauty not to change or wither in the future, then, though the joy of love may have its evil, still it might hold the mind in thraldom. To know that other men grow old, and sicken, and die, would be enough to rob such joys of satisfaction: yet how much more in their own case (knowing this) would discontentment fill the mind; to know such pleasures hasten to decay, and their bodies likewise; if, notwithstanding this, men yield to the power of love, their case indeed is like the very beasts. It is but to seduce one with a hollow lie. Alas! alas! Udayi! these, after all, are the great concerns; the pain of birth, old age, disease, and death; this grief is what we have to fear; the eyes see all things falling to decay, and yet the heart finds joy in following them. Alas! for all the world! how dark and ignorant, void of understanding!"

And he made this vow: "I now will seek a noble law, unlike the worldly methods known to men. I will oppose disease and age and death, and strive against the mischief wrought by these on men." To do this he resolved to leave the palace for good and go meditate in the solitude of the forest, as was the custom in those days of natural religion.

And he pointed out the sleeping girls to Udayi, for they

were no longer beautiful with their lamentable tricks laid aside, snoring, sprawled all over in different ungainly positions, mere pitiful sisters now in the sorrow-burning globe.

When the king heard of his son's decision to leave home and take up the holy life, he protested tearfully. But the young monarch said: "O! place no difficulties in my path; your son is dwelling in a burning house, would you indeed prevent his leaving it! To solve doubt is only reasonable, who could forbid a man to seek its explanation?" And he made it clear that he would rather take his life than to be held by filial duty to go on in ignorance.

Seeing his father crying the Prince decided to make his departure by night. Not only the Maharajah but the beautiful princess Yasodhara was beseeching him not to renounce the duties and responsibilities of royal reign and of married life. With his head in Yasodhara's lap he inwardly grieved, knowing the suffering that his full renunciation would cause her. And he pondered: "My loving mother when she bore me, with deep affection painfully carried me, and then when born she died, not permitted to nourish me. One alive, the other dead, gone by different roads, where now shall she be found? Like as in a wilderness, on some high tree, all the birds living with their mates assemble in the evening and at dawn disperse, so are the separations of the world." Looking at his three-year-old son Rahula, the thoughts dawned that he would utter later: "Call his name Rahula, a bond, for here is another bond which I must break."

To Kandaka his servant, in the mid watches of the night when everything was ready, he said, "Saddle then my horse, and quickly bring it here. I wish to reach the deathless city; my heart is fixed beyond all change, resolved I am and bound by sacred oath."

Quietly they rode out the royal gate. Looking back once, the trembling Prince cried: "If I escape not birth, old age, and death, for evermore I pass not thus along."

Master and servant rode through the forest of the night. At dawn, arriving at a spot, they dismounted and rested. "You have borne me well!" said the Prince patting his horse. And to his servant: "Ever have you followed after me when riding, and deeply have I felt my debt of thanks—I only knew you as a man truehearted—But with many words I cannot hold you here, so let me say in brief to you, we have now ended our relationship: take, then, my horse and ride back again; for me, during the long night past, that place I sought to reach now I have obtained!"

Seeing that the servant was full of reluctance and remorse, the Prince handed him a precious jewel. "O Kandaka, take this gem, and going back to where my father is, take the jewel and lay it reverently before him, to signify my heart's relation to him: and then, for me, request the king to stifle every fickle feeling of affection, and say that I, to escape from birth and age and death, have entered on the wild forest of painful discipline; not that I may get a heavenly birth, much less because I have no tenderness of heart, or that I cherish any cause of bitterness but only that I seek the way of ultimate escape.

"My very ancestors, victorious kings, thinking their throne established and immovable, have handed down to me their kingly wealth; I, thinking only on religion, put it all away; I rejoice to have acquired religious wealth.

"And if you say that I am young and tender, and that the time for seeking is not come, you ought to know that to seek true religion, there is never a time not fit; impermanence and fickleness, the hate of death, these ever follow us, and therefore I embrace the present day, convinced that now is the time to seek."

Poor Kandaka cried.

"You should overcome this sorrowful mood, it is for you to comfort yourself; all creatures, each in its way, foolishly arguing that all things are constant, would influence me today not to forsake my kin and relatives; but when dead and come to be a ghost, how then, let them say, can I be kept?"

These were words of a potential, dazzling, pure Sage yet coming from the lips of a youthful and gentle prince they were like weights of sorrow to those who loved him and coveted his

continuing regard. But there was no other way; his relationship
with the world had to be snapped.

"People from the beginning have erred thus," he said, "binding themselves in society and by the ties of love and then, as
after a dream, all is dispersed. You may make known my words,
'When I have escaped from the sad ocean of birth and death,
then afterwards I will come back again; but I am resolved, if I
obtain not my quest, my body shall perish in the mountain
wilds.'"

Then he took his glittering sword and cut off his beautiful
golden hair, and attached the sword together with some precious jewels to the saddle of his swift footed war horse: "Follow
closely after Kandaka. Do not let sorrow rise within, I grieve
indeed at losing you, my gallant steed. Your merit now has
gained its end: you shall enjoy for long a respite from an evil
birth." And off he clapped them, servant and horse, and stood
alone in the forest, bare headed, empty handed, like a Vajra-god
ready and waiting yet already victorious.

"My adornments now are gone forever, there only now remain these silken garments, which are not in keeping with a
hermit's life."

A man passed by in ragged clothes. Gotama called out,
"That dress of thine belikes me much, as if it were not foul, and
this my dress I'll give thee in exchange." The man, whom Got-

ama took to be a hunter, was actually a religious hermit, or Rishi, a Sage, a Muni. The Prince soon surmised this as soon as the transfer of clothes was effected. "This garment is of no common character! It is not what a worldly man has worn."

He wandered on, deep in earnestness. Late in the day he grew very hungry. In the tradition of old, vowed to homelessness, he begged his first meal from door to door among the village grass huts. Having been a prince he was used to the best dishes that royal chefs could prepare, and so now when these offerings of humble food met his educated palate he instinctively began spitting it out. Instantly he realized the patheticness of this folly and forced himself to eat the entire bowlful. Whatever was given to him in charity, though it may be wretched, should never be despised. The religious life dedicated to the search for the highest peace, having the one savor of reality, was seasoning enough indeed. Having cast off worldly ties of the heart and thinking mind, it was no time to be tied to the tasting tongue. Having eaten the humbling, the dreary meal, downcast yet joyful, he who had worn garments of silk and whose attendants had held a white umbrella over him, walked on in rags in the burning sunshine of the jungle solitude.

He made inquiries and roamed along looking for the famous ascetic, Alara Kalama, whom he'd heard so much about, who would be his teacher. Alara Kalama expounded the teaching called "the realm of nothingness," and practiced self-mortification to prove that he was free from his body. The young new Muni of the Sakya clan followed suit with eagerness and energy. Later, to his disciples, he recounted these early experiences of a self-mortifyer. "I fed my body on mosses, grasses, cow-dung, I lived upon the wild fruits and roots of the jungle, eating only of fruit fallen from the trees. I wore garments of hemp and hair, as also foul clouts from the charnel house, rags from dust heaps. I wrapped myself in the abandoned skins and hides of animals; covered my nakedness with lengths of grass, bark and leaves, with a patch of some wild animal's mane or tail, with the wing of an owl. I was also a plucker out of hair and beard, practiced the austerity of rooting out hair from head and face. I took upon myself the vow always to stand, never to sit or lie down. I bound myself perpetually to squat upon my heels, practiced the austerity of continual heel-squatting. A 'thorn-sided-one' was I; when I lay down to rest, it was with thorns upon my sides— I betook myself to a certain dark and dreadful wood and in that place made my abode. And here in the dense and fearsome forest such horror reigned, that the hair of whomsoever, not sense-subdued, entered that dread place, stood on end with terror." For six years with Alara Kalama and later the five mendicant hermits near Uruvela in the Forest of Mortification he who would become the Buddha practiced these useless and grisly exercises together with a penance of starvation so severe that "like wasted withered reeds became all my limbs, like a camel's hoof my hips, like a wavy rope my backbone, and as in a ruined house the rooftree rafters show all aslope, so sloping showed my ribs because of the extremity of fasting. And when I touched the surface of my belly my hand touched my backbone, and as I stroked my limbs the hair, rotten at the roots, came away in my hands."

Finally one day in trying to bathe in the Nairanjana he fainted in the water and almost drowned. He realized that this extreme method of finding salvation was just another form of pitiful ignorance; he saw it was the other side of the coin of existence that on one side showed extreme lusting, the other extreme fasting; extreme luxurious concupiscence and sense-enervation on the one hand, dulling the heart of sincerity, and extreme impoverished duress and body-deprivation on the other hand, also dulling the heart of sincerity from the other side of the same arbitrary and cause-benighted action.

"Pitiful indeed are such sufferings!" he cried, on being revived by a bowlful of rice milk donated to him by a maiden who thought he was a god. Going to the five ascetic hermits he preached at last: "You! to obtain the joys of heaven, promoting the destruction of your outward form, and undergoing every kind of painful penance, and yet seeking to obtain another birth—seeking a birth in heaven, to suffer further trouble, seeing visions of future joy, while the heart sinks with feebleness . . . I should therefore rather seek strength of body, by drink and food refresh my members, with contentment cause my mind to rest. My mind at rest, I shall enjoy silent composure. Composure is the trap for getting ecstasy; while in ecstasy perceiving the true law, disentanglement will follow.

"I desire to escape from the three worlds—all earth, heaven and hell. The law which you practice, you inherit from the deeds of former teachers, but I, desiring to destroy all combination, seek a law which admits of no such accident. And, therefore, I cannot in this grove delay for a longer while in fruitless discussions."

The mendicants were shocked and said that Gotama had given up. But Sakyamuni, calling their way "trying to tie the air into knots," ceased to be a tapasa self-torturer and became a paribbijaka wanderer.

Wayfaring, he heard of his father's grief, after six years so keen, and his gentle heart was affected with increased love. "But yet," he told his newsbearer, "all is like the fancy of a dream, quickly reverting to nothingness . . . Family love, ever being bound, ever being loosened, who can sufficiently lament such constant separations? All things which exist in time must perish . . . Because, then, death pervades all time, get rid of death, and time will disappear . . .

"You desire to make me king . . . Thinking anxiously of the outward form, the spirit droops . . . The sumptuously ornamented and splendid palace I look upon as filled with fire; the hundred dainty dishes of the divine kitchen, as mingled with destructive poisons. Illustrious kings in sorrowful disgust know the troubles of a royal estate are not to be compared with the repose of a religious life. Escape is born from quietness and rest. Royalty and rescue, motion and rest, cannot be united. My mind is not uncertain; severing the baited hook of relationship, with straightforward purpose, I have left my home.

"Follow the pure law of self denial," he preached on the road to other hermits. "Reflect on what was said of old. Sin is the cause of grief." The glorious Asvhaghosha describes the Buddha, at this stage: "With even gait and unmoved presence he entered on the town and begged his food, according to the rule of all great hermits, with joyful mien and undisturbed mind, not anxious whether much or little alms were given; whatever he received, costly or poor, he placed within his bowl, then turned back to the wood, and having eaten it and drunk of the flowing stream, he joyous sat upon the immaculate mountain."

And he spoke to kings and converted them. "The wealth of a country is not constant treasure but that which is given in charity," he told King Bimbisara of Magadha who had come to him in the woods asking why a man of royal birth should give up the advantages of rule. "Charity scatters, yet it brings no repentance."

But the King wanted to know, Why should a wise man, knowing these valuable injunctions concerning rule, give up the throne and deprive himself of the comforts of palace life?

"I fear birth, old age, disease and death, and so I seek to find a sure mode of deliverance. And so I fear the five desires—the desires attached to seeing, hearing, tasting, smelling, and touching—the inconstant thieves, stealing from men their choicest treasures, making them unreal, false and fickle—the great obstacles, forever disarranging the way of peace.

"If the joys of heaven are not worth having, how much less the desires common to men, begetting the thirst of wild love, and then lost in the enjoyment. Like a king who rules all within the four seas, yet still seeks beyond for something more, so is desire, so is lust; like the unbounded ocean, it knows not when and where to stop. Indulge in lust a little, and like the child it grows apace. The wise man seeing the bitterness of sorrow, stamps out and destroys the risings of desire.

"That which the world calls virtue is another form of the sorrowful law.

"Recollecting that all things are illusory, the wise man covets them not; he who desires such things, desires sorrow.

"The wise man casts away the approach of sorrow as a rotten bone.

"That which the wise man will not take, the king will go through fire and water to obtain, a labor for wealth as for a piece of putrid flesh.

"So riches, the wise man is ill-pleased at having wealth stored up, the mind wild with anxious thoughts, guarding himself by night and day, as a man who fears some powerful enemy.

"How painfully do men scheme after wealth, difficult to acquire, easy to dissipate, as that which is got in a dream; how can the wise man hoard up such trash! It is this which makes a man vile, and lashes and goads him with piercing sorrow; lust debases a man, robs him of all hope, while through the long night his body and soul are worn out.

"It is like the fish that covets the baited hook.

"Greediness seeks for something to satisfy its longings, but, there is no permanent cessation of sorrow; for by coveting to appease these desires we only increase them. Time passes and the sorrow recurs.

"Though a man be concerned in ten thousand matters, what profit is there in this, for we only accumulate anxieties. Put an end to sorrow then, by appeasing desire, refrain from busy work, this is rest."

But King Bimbisara could not help remarking as Kandaka had done, that the Prince of the Sakyas was so young to renounce the world.

"You say that while young a man should be gay, and when old then religious, but I regard the fickleness of age as bringing with it loss of power to be religious unlike the firmness and power of youth."

The old king understood.

"Inconstancy is the great hunter, age his bow, disease his arrows, in the fields of life and death he hunts for living things as for the deer; when he gets his opportunity he takes our life; who then would wait for age?"

And with respect to religious determination he counselled the king to stay away from the practice of sacrifices. "Destroying life to gain religious merit, what love can such a man possess? even if the reward of such sacrifices were lasting, even for this, slaughter would be unseemly; how much more when the reward is transient! The wise avoid destroying life! Future reward and the promised fruit, these are governed by transient, fickle laws, like the wind, or the drop that is blown from the grass; such things therefore I put away from me, and I seek for true escape."

The king realized that his understanding was more important than his wealth, because it came before. He thought: "May

I keep the law, the time for understanding is short." He became an enlightened ruler and lifelong supporter of Gotama.

Gotama conducted learned discussions with hermit leaders in the forest. Of Arada Udarama he asked: "With respect to old age, disease, and death, how are these things to be escaped?"

The hermit replied that by the "I" being rendered pure, forthwith there was true deliverance. This was the ancient teaching propounding the Immortal Soul, the "Purusha," Atman, the Oversoul that went from life to life getting more and more or less and less pure, with its final goal pure soulhood in heaven. But the holy intelligence of Gotama perceived that this "Purusha" was no better than a ball being bounced around according to concomitant circumstances, whether in heaven, hell, or on earth, and as long as one held this view there was no perfect escape from birth and destruction of birth. The birth of any thing means death of the thing: and this is decay, this is horror, change, this is pain.

Spoke Gotama: "You say that the 'I' being rendered pure, forthwith there is true deliverance; but if we encounter a union of cause and effect, then there is a return to the trammels of birth; just as the germ in the seed, when earth, fire, water, and wind seem to have destroyed in it the principle of life, meeting with favorable concomitant circumstances, will yet revive, without any evident cause, but because of desire, and just to die again; so those who have gained this supposed release, likewise keeping the idea of 'I' and living things, have in fact gained no final deliverance."

Approaching now his moment of perfection in wisdom and compassion the young Saint saw all things, men sitting in groves, trees, sky, different views about the soul, different selves, as one unified emptiness in the air, one imaginary flower, the significance of which was unity and undividable-ness, all of the same dreamstuff, universal and secretly pure.

He saw that existence was like the light of a candle: the light of the candle and the extinction of the light of the candle were the same thing.

He saw that there was no need to conceive the existence of any Oversoul, as if to predicate the entity of any ball, to have it be bounced around according to the winds of the harsh imaginary March of things, and all of it a mind-made mess, much as a dreamer continues his nightmare on purpose hoping to extricate himself from the frightful difficulties that he doesn't realize are only in his mind.

Gotama saw the peace of the Buddha's Nirvana. Nirvana means blown out, as of a candle. But because the Buddha's Nirvana is beyond existence, and conceives neither the existence or non-existence of the light of a candle, or an immortal soul, or any <u>thing</u>, it is not even Nirvana, it is neither the light of the candle known as Sangsara (this world) nor the blown-out extinction of the light of the candle known as Nirvana (the no-world) but awake beyond these arbitrarily established conceptions.

He was not satisfied with Arada's idea of the "I" being cleared and purified for heaven. He saw no "I" in the matter. Nothing to be purified. And covetous of heaven nothing but activity in a dream. He knew that when seen from the point of view of the true mind, all things were like magic castles in the air.

"What Arada has declared cannot satisfy my heart. I must go and seek a better explanation."

Gotama was about to find that explanation. As an eminent writer said: "He had sought for it in man and nature, and found it not, and lo! it was in his own heart!"

The blessed hermit went to Budhgaya. At once the ancient dream of the Buddhas of Old possessed him as he gazed at the noble groves of palm and mango and <u>ficus religiosa</u> fig trees; in the rippling afternoon he passed beneath their branches, lonely and bemused, yet with a stirring of premonition in his heart that something great was about to happen here. Gotama the "founder" of Buddhism was only rediscovering the lost and ancient path of the Tathagata (He of Suchnesshood); re-unfolding the primal dew drop of the world; like the swan of pity descending in the lotus pool, and settling, great joy overwhelmed him at the sight of the tree which he chose to sit under as per agreement with all the Buddha-lands and assembled Buddha-things which are No-things in the emptiness of sparkling intuition all around like swarms of angels and Bodhisattvas in mothlike density radiating endlessly towards the center of the void in ADORATION. "Everywhere is Here," intuited the saint. From yonder man, a grass cutter, he obtained some pure and pliant grass, which spreading out beneath the tree, with upright body, there he took his seat; his feet placed under him, not carelessly arranged, moving to and fro, but like the firmly fixed and compact Naga god. "I WILL NOT RISE FROM THIS SPOT," he resolved within himself, "UNTIL, FREED FROM CLINGING, MY MIND ATTAINS TO DELIVERANCE FROM ALL SORROW."

His bones could rot and his sinew shrivel, and crows pick on his abandoned brain, but this godlike man would not rise from this spot on the bed of grass beneath the fig tree until he had solved the riddle of the world. He set his teeth and pressed his tongue against them. He bent his radiant intelligence down, and let his consciousness drift into the inner intuition of insight. Hands folded gently, breathing like a baby, eyes closed, immovable and undisturbable, he intuited, as dusk descended on the terrace of the earth whereon he sat. "Though all the earth be moved and shaken, yet would this place be fixed and stable."

It was May in India, the time known as Cowdust, when the air is golden as grain, warm and dreamy, and all things and beasts breathe forth their faith in sundowns of natural mental quiet.

Many words have been written about this holy moment in the now famous spot beneath this Bodhi-Tree, or Wisdom-Tree. It was not an agony in the garden, it was a bliss beneath the tree; it was not the resurrection of anything, but the annihilation of all things. Came to Buddha in those hours the realization that all things come from a cause and go to dissolution, and therefore all things are impermanent, all things are unhappy, and thereby and most mysterious, all things are unreal.

A cool refreshing breeze rose as he realized everything had flowered out of the mind, sprung from the seeds of false thinking in the Divine Ground of Reality, and there stood the dream all woeful and in gloom. "Beasts, quiet and silent, looked on in wonderment." Temptations filled the mind of the Buddha to rise and go elsewhere and give up this futile meditating under trees; he recognized these temptations as the work of the very Tempter, Mara, the Indian Devil, and refused to budge. Even fear crossed his brain, imaginary fevers that something was going on behind his back, before his closed eyes: unmoved like a man watching children at play, he let these doubts and disturbances, like bubbles, vanish back to their origin in the emptiness of the mental sea.

By nightfall he reposed peaceful and quiet. He entered into

deep and subtle contemplation. Every kind of holy ecstasy in order passed before his eyes. During the first watch of the night he entered on "right perception" and in recollection all former births passed before his eyes.

"Born in such a place, of such a name, and downwards to his present birth, so through hundreds, thousands, myriads, all his births and deaths he knew."

Knowing full well that the essence of existence is of one suchness, what birth could not his Bright, Mysterious, Intuitive Essence of Mind recall? As though he had been all things, and only because there had never been a true "he," but all things, and so all things were the same thing, and it was within the purview of the Universal Mind, which was the Only Mind past, present, and future.

"Countless as the sands of the Ganges were the births and deaths, of every kind and sort; then knowing, too, his family relationships, great pity rose within his heart."

It had been a long time already finished, the ancient dream of life, the tears of the many-mothered sadness, the myriads of fathers in the dust, eternities of lost afternoons of sisters and brothers, the sleepy cock crow, the insect cave, the pitiful instinct all wasted on emptiness, the great huge drowsy Golden Age sensation that opened in his brain that this knowledge was older than the world.

"The sense of deep compassion passed, he once again considered 'all that lives' and how they moved within the six portions of life's revolution, no final term to birth and death; hollow all, and false and transient as the plantain tree, or as a dream, or phantasy."

In the ears of the Buddha as he thus sat in brilliant and sparkling craft of intuition, so that light like Transcendental Milk dazzled in the invisible dimness of his closed eyelids, was heard the unvarying pure hush of the sighing sea of hearing, seething, receding, as he more or less recalled the consciousness of the sound, though in itself it was always the same steady sound, only his consciousness of it varied and receded, like low tide flats and the salty water sizzling and sinking in the sand, the sound neither outside nor within the ear but everywhere, the pure sea of hearing, the Transcendental Sound of Nirvana heard by children in cribs and on the moon and in the heart of howling storms, and in which the young Buddha now heard a teaching going on, a ceaseless instruction wise and clear from all the Buddhas of Old that had come before him and all the Buddhas a-Coming. Beneath the distant cricket howl occasional noises like the involuntary peep of sleeping dream birds, or scutters of little fieldmice, or a vast breeze in the trees disturbed the peace of this Hearing but the noises were merely accidental, the Hearing received all noises and accidents in its sea but remained as ever undisturbed, truly unpenetrated, and neither replenished nor diminished, as self-pure as empty space. Under the blazing stars the King of the Law, enveloped in the divine tranquillity of this Transcendental Sound of the Diamond Ecstasy, rested moveless.

"Then in the middle watch of night, he reached to knowledge of the pure Angels, and beheld before him every creature, as one sees images upon a mirror; all creatures born and born again to die, noble and mean, the poor and rich, reaping the fruit of right or evil doing, and sharing happiness or misery in consequence."

He saw how evil deeds leave cause for regret and the nameless desire to redress and re-straighten badness, initiating energy for return to the stage of the world: whereas good deeds, producing no remorse and leaving no substratum of doubt, vanish into Enlightenment.

"He saw, moreover, all the fruits of birth as beasts; some doomed to die for the sake of skin or flesh, some for their horns or hair or bones or wings; others torn or killed in mutual conflict, friend or relative before; some burdened with loads or dragging heavy weights, others pierced or urged on by pricking goads. Blood flowing down their tortured forms, parched and hungry—no relief afforded, one with the other struggling, possessed of no independent strength. Flying through the air or sunk in deep water, yet no place as a refuge left from death.

"And he saw those reborn as men, with bodies like some foul sewer, ever moving among the direst sufferings, born from the womb to fear and trembling, with body tender, touching anything its feelings painful, as if cut with knives."

This valley of darts, which we call life, a nightmare.

"Whilst born in this condition, no moment free from chance of death, labor, and sorrow, yet seeking birth again, and being born again, enduring pain."

The millstone of the pitiful forms of ignorance rolling and grinding on and on.

"Then he saw those who by a higher merit were enjoying heaven; a thirst for love ever consuming them, their merit ended with the end of life, the five signs warning them of death. Just as the blossom that decays, withering away, is robbed of all its shining tints; not all their associates, living still, through grieving, can avail to save the rest. The palaces and joyous precincts empty now, the Angels all alone and desolate, sitting or asleep upon the dusty earth, weep bitterly in recollection of their loves. Deceived, alas! no single place exempt, in every birth incessant pain!

"Heaven, hell, or earth, the sea of birth and death revolving thus—an ever-whirling wheel—all flesh immersed within its waves cast here and there without reliance! Thus with his Mind eyes he thoughtfully considered the five domains of life and the degradation of all creatures that are born. He saw that all was empty and vain alike! with no dependence! like the plantain or the bubble."

The groundmist of 3 A.M. rose with all the dolors of the world. "On the third eventful watch he entered on the deep, true apprehension. He meditated on the entire world of crea- tures, whirling in life's tangle, born to sorrow: the crowds who live, grow old, and die, immeasurable for multitude. Covetous, lustful, ignorant, darkly-fettered, with no way known for final rescue."

O what was the cause of all this death of bodies? "Rightly considering, inwardly he reflected from what source birth and death proceed."

Birth of bodies is the direct cause of death of bodies. Just as, implantation of its seed was the cause of the cast off rose.

Then looking further, Where does birth come from? he saw it came from life-deeds done elsewhere; then scanning those deeds, he saw they were not framed by a creator, not self caused, nor personal existences nor were they either uncaused; he saw they themselves obtained along a further chain of causes, cause upon cause, concatenative links joining the fetters binding all that is form—poor form, mere dust and pain.

Then, as one who breaks the first bamboo joint finds all the rest easy to separate, having discerned the cause of death as birth, and the cause of birth as deeds, he gradually came to see the truth; <u>death</u> comes from <u>birth</u>, <u>birth</u> comes from <u>deeds</u>, <u>deeds</u> come from <u>attachment</u>, <u>attachment</u> comes from <u>de-sire</u>, <u>desire</u> comes from <u>perception</u>, <u>perception</u> comes from <u>sen-sation</u>, <u>sensation</u> comes from <u>the six sense organs</u>, <u>the six sense organs</u> come from <u>individuality</u>, <u>individuality</u> comes from <u>con-sciousness</u>. Deeds come from attachment, deeds are done for a reason of imagined need to which a being has become attached and in the name of which he's made his move; attachment comes from desire, the desire comes before the habit; desire comes from perception, you never desired something you didn't know about, and when you did, it was a perception of either pleasure which you desired, or pain which you loathed with aversion, both being two sides of the coin named desire; percep-tion came from sensation, the sensation of a burning finger is not perceived at once; sensation came because of the contact of the six sense organs (eye-seeing, ear-hearing, nose-smelling, tongue-tasting, body-feeling and brain-thinking) with their mu-tual objects of sense, as, no finger is burned that has never con-tacted the flame; six sense organs come because of individuality, just as the germ grows to the stem and leaf, individuality grow-ing its own sixfold division of what was originally neither One nor Six but Pure Mind, mirror-clear; individuality comes because of consciousness, consciousness like the seed that germinates and brings forth its individual leaf, and if not consciousness then where is the leaf?; consciousness in turn, proceeds from individuality, the two are intervolved leaving no remnant; by some concurrent cause consciousness engenders individuality, while by some other cause concurrent, individuality engenders consciousness. Just as a man and ship advance together, the water and the land mutually involved; thus consciousness brings forth individuality; individuality produces the roots. The roots engender contact of the six sense organs; contact again brings forth sensation; sensation brings forth desire (or aversion); desire or aversion produce attachment to either desire or aversion; this attachment is the cause of deeds; and deeds again engender birth; birth again produces death; so does this one incessant round cause the existence of all living things.

And beyond this, instantly viewing and completing the Twelve Links in the Chain of Existence (the Nirdana Chain), he saw that this consciousness which brings forth individuality together with all this trouble, itself comes from Karma (leftover unfinished action of the dream), and Karma comes from Ignorance, and Ignorance comes from Mind. Karma is the impersonation of the inexorable, inflexible law that bound together act and result, this life and the next; Karma explains everything that concerns the world of living beings, animals, men, the power of kings, the physical beauty of women, the splendid tail of pea-cocks, the moral dispositions of everyone; Karma is a sentient being's inheritance, the womb which bears him or it, the womb to which he or it must resort; Karma is the root of morality, for, what we have been makes us what we are now. If a man becomes enlightened, stops, and realizes highest perfect wisdom and en-ters Nirvana, it is because his Karma had worked itself out and it was in his Karma to do so; if a man goes on in ignorance, angry, foolish and greedy, it is because his Karma had not yet worked itself out and it was in his Karma to do so.

Rightly illumined, thoroughly perceiving, firmly established, thus was he enlightened.

Destroy birth, thus death will cease; destroy deeds then will birth cease; destroy attachment then will deeds cease; destroy desire then will attachment end; destroy perception then will desire end; destroy sensation then ends perception; destroy con-tact of the six sense organs then ends sensation; the six en-trances of the sense organs all destroyed, from this, moreover, individuality and the picking out of different related notions will cease. Consciousness destroyed, individuality will cease; indi-viduality destroyed, then consciousness perishes; consciousness ended, the dream energy of Karma has no hold and handle; Karma done, ignorance of dreaming ends; ignorance destroyed, then the constituents of individual life will die: the Great Rishi was thus perfected in wisdom.

Here is the list of the Nirdana Chain Links:

1. Ignorance
2. Karma
3. Consciousness
4. Individuality
5. Six contact organs
6. Sensation
7. Perception
8. Desire
9. Attachment
10. Deeds
11. Birth
12. Death

Insight arose, ignorance was dispelled; darkness was done away and light dawned. Thus sat the Buddha of our present world, strenuous, aglow, and master of himself, singing this song in his heart:

"Many a house of life has held me;
Long have I struggled to find him
Who made these sorrowful prisons of the senses!

But now, you builder of this tabernacle—You!
I know thee! Never shall you build again
These walls of pain, nor raise the roof-tree
Of deceits, nor lay fresh rafters on the clay;
Broken your house is! and the ridgepole split!
Delusion fashioned it! Ignorance is your name!
Safe I pass now, deliverance to obtain."

In him, thus freed, arose knowledge and freedom, and he knew that rebirth was at an end, and that the goal had been reached.

And for the benefit of the world he now devised the way, based on the Four Noble Truths.

THE FOUR NOBLE TRUTHS

1. All life is suffering . . . (all existence is in a state of misery, impermanency and unreality.)
2. The cause of suffering is ignorant craving
3. The suppression of suffering can be achieved
4. The way is the noble eightfold path.
   And the Noble Eightfold Path is as follows:

THE NOBLE EIGHTFOLD PATH

1. <u>Right Ideas</u>, based on these Four Noble Truths
2. <u>Right Resolution</u> to follow this Way out of the suffering

3. <u>Right Speech</u>, tender sorrowful discourse with the brothers and sisters of the world

4. <u>Right Behavior</u>, gentle, helpful, chaste conduct everywhere

5. <u>Right Means of Livelihood</u>, harmless foodgathering is your living

6. <u>Right Effort</u>, rousing oneself with energy and zeal to this Holy Way

7. <u>Right Mindfulness</u>, keeping in mind the dangers of the other way (of the world)

8. <u>Right Meditation</u>, practicing Solitary meditation and prayer to attain holy ecstasy and spiritual graces for the sake of the enlightenment of all sentient beings (practicing Dhyana to attain Samadhi and Samapatti).

"When this knowledge had arisen within me, my heart and mind were freed from the drug of lust, from the drug of rebirth, from the drug of ignorance."

Thus did he complete the end of "self," as fire goes out for want of grass; thus he had done what he would have men do; he had found the way of perfect knowledge. And he knew as he sat there lustrous with all wisdom, perfect in gifts, that the way of perfect knowledge had been handed down to him from Buddhas Innumerable of Old that had come before in all ten directions of all ten quarters of the universe where he now saw them in a mighty vision assembled in brightness and power sitting on their intrinsic thrones in the Glorious Lotus Blossoms everywhere throughout phenomena and space and forever giving response to the needs of all sentient life in all the kingdoms of existence, past, present, and future.

With the discernment of the grand truths and their realization in life the Rishi became enlightened; he thus attained Sambodhi (Perfect Wisdom) and became a Buddha. Rightly has Sambodhi been called, it can be accomplished only by self help without the extraneous aid of a teacher or a god. As the poet says,

> "Save his own soul's light overhead
> None leads man, none ever led."

The morning sunbeams brightened with the dawn, the dustlike mist dispersing, disappeared. The moon and stars paled their faint light, the barriers of the night were all removed. He had finished this the first great lesson and the final lesson and the lesson of old; entering the great Rishi's house of Dreamless Sleep, fixed in holy trance, he had reached the source of exhaustless truth, the happiness that never ends and that had no beginning but was always already there within the True Mind.

Not by anxious use of outward means, had Buddha unveiled the True Mind and ended suffering, but by resting quietly in thoughtful silence. This is the supreme fact of blessed rest.

He was <u>sihibhuto</u>, cooled.

Now arrived the most critical moment in the life of the Blessed One. After many struggles he had found the most profound truths, truths teeming with meaning but comprehensible only by the wise, truths full of blessing but difficult to make out by ordinary minds. Mankind were worldly and hankering for pleasure. Though they possessed the capacity for religious knowledge and virtue and could perceive the true nature of things, they rushed to do other things and got entangled in deceptive thoughts in the net of ignorance, like puppet dolls that were made to jiggle according to some ignorant opposing arbitrary ideas that had nothing to do with their own essential and enlightened stillness. Could they comprehend the law of Karma-retribution automatically left over from previous deed-dreams, or the law of continuous connection of cause and effect in the moral world? Could they rid themselves of the animistic idea of a soul and grasp the true nature of man? Could they overcome the propensity to seek salvation through a mediatorial caste of priests and brahmins? Could they understand the final state of peace, that quenching of all worldly cravings which leads to the blissful haven of Nirvana? Would it be advisable for him in these circumstances to preach to all mankind the truths he had discovered? Might not failure result in anguish and pain? Such were the doubts and questions which arose in his mind, but only to be smothered and quenched by thoughts of universal compassion. He who had abandoned all selfishness could not but live for others. What could be a better way of living for others than to show them the path of attaining perfect bliss? What could be greater service to mankind than to rescue the struggling creatures engulfed in the mournful sea of this Sangsaric world of pain and debris? Is not the gift of Dharma, the "Established Law," the transparent crystal clearness of the world, the greatest of all gifts? The Perfect One looked up at that king of trees with an unwavering gaze. "This law is wonderful and lofty," he considered in his heart, "whereas creatures are blind with dulness and ignorance. What shall I do? At the very time that I am uttering syllables, beings are oppressed with evils. In their ignorance they will not heed the law I announce, and in consequence of it they will incur some penalty. It would be better were I never to speak. May my quiet extinction take place this very day."

But on remembering the former Buddhas and their skillfulness in all kinds of worlds, in instructing various beings to realize the perfect simple truth: "Nay, I also will manifest the Buddha-enlightenment."

To Sariputra and a vast and reverent assembly of saints, Gotama thus recalled his hours under the Bo-Tree: "When I was thus meditating on the law the other Buddhas in all directions of space appeared to me in their own body and raised their voice, crying 'Om! Amen, Solitary, first leader of the world! Now that thou hast come to unsurpassed knowledge, and art meditating on the skillfulness of the leaders of the world, thou repeatest their teaching. We also, being Buddhas, will make clear the highest word, divided into three bodies (Appearance-body, Bliss-body, and Law-body): for men have low inclinations, and might perchance from ignorance not believe, 'Ye shall become Buddhas.'

" 'Hence we will arouse many Wise Beings (Bodhisattva-Manasattvas) by the display of skillfulness and the encouraging of the wish of obtaining fruits.'

"And I was delighted to hear the sweet voice of the leaders of men: in the exultation of my heart I said to the blessed saints, 'The words of the eminent sages are not spoken in vain.'

" 'I, too, will act according to the indications of the wise leaders of the world; having myself been born in the midst of the degradation of creatures, I have known agitation in this dreadful world.'

"Then I conceived the idea that the time had come for me to announce the excellent law and to reveal supreme enlightenment, for which task I had been born in the world.

"At certain times, at certain places, somehow do the leaders appear in the world, and after their appearance will they, whose view is boundless, at one time or another preach a similar law.

"It is most difficult to meet with this superior law, even in the myriads of ten millions of Aeons; very rare are the creatures that will adhere to the superior law which they have heard from the Buddhas.

"Just as the blossom of the glomerous fig-tree is rare, albeit sometimes, at some places, and somehow it is met with, as something pleasant to see for everybody, as a wonder to the world including the gods.

"And far more wonderful is the law I proclaim. Anyone who, on hearing a good exposition of it, shall cheerfully accept it and recite but one word of it, will have done honor to all the Buddhas.

"Give up all doubt and uncertainty in this respect: I declare that I am Dharma-Raja, the King of the Law.

"You shall become Buddhas; rejoice!"

Thus Tathagata, He-Who-Has-Attained-to-Suchness-of-Mind and sees no more differentiation of various creatures and phenomena, who entertains no more definite conceptions of self, other selves, many divided selves, or one undivided universal self, to whom the world is no longer noticeable, except as a pitiful apparition, yet without arbitrary conception either of its existence or non-existence, as one thinks not to measure the

substantiality of a dream but only to wake from it; thus Tathagata, piously composed and silent, radiant with glory, shedding
light around, rose from under his Tree of Enlightenment, and
with unmatched dignity advanced alone over the dreamlike earth
as if surrounded by a crowd of followers, thinking, "To fulfill my
ancient oath, to rescue all not yet delivered, I will follow out
my ancient vow. Let those that have ears to hear master the
noble path of salvation."

He headed for Benares, the capital of the world.

On the road he ran into a former acquaintance, Upaka, a
naked Jain monk, who, struck by the majestical and joyful appearance of the human being who had just singlehandedly remembered the origin of the world and by striking down the
forgotten path had renewed the ancient vow that had been a
long time already hidden in the world like the jewel in the lotus,
inquired: "Who is the teacher under whose guidance you have
renounced the world?"

"I have no master," replied the Enlightened One, "no honor-
able tribe; no point of excellence; self-taught in this profoundest
doctrine, I have arrived at superhuman wisdom.

"Through all Benares soon will sound the drum of life,
no stay is possible—I have no name—nor do I seek profit or
pleasure.

"That which behooves the world to learn, but throughout

the world no learner found, I now myself and by myself have learned completely; 'tis rightly called Perfect Wisdom.

"That hateful family of griefs the sword of wisdom has destroyed, this then is what the world has named and rightly named, the 'Chiefest Victory.'"

And he said: "I have no master. To me there is no equal. I am the perfect one, the Buddha. I have attained peace. I have obtained Nirvana. To found the Kingdom of righteousness I am going to Benares. There I shall light the Bright Lamp for the benefit of those who are shrouded in the gloomy darkness of life and death."

"Do you profess to be the conqueror of the world?" demanded the monk.

The Awakened One replied: "Conquerors of the world are those who have conquered self, those alone are victors who control their passions and abstain from sin. I have conquered self and overcome all sin. Therefore am I the conqueror of the world.

"Like as the lamp shines in the dark, without a purpose of its own, self-radiant, so burns the lamp of the Tathagata, without the shadow of a personal feeling."

And he moved on to Benares.

There, in the deer park Isipatana, sat the five mendicant ascetics with whom he'd spent those futile six years in the Forest of Mortification. They saw him coming, slowly, his eyes cast down with circumspection and modesty a plough's length along the ground as if he was ploughing and planting the Ambrosial crop of the law as he went. They scoffed.

"There comes Gotama who broke his first vow by giving up ascetic practices and mortification. Don't rise in salutation, give him an offhand greeting, don't offer him the customary refreshments when he comes."

However, when the Buddha approached them in a dignified manner, they involuntarily arose from their seats, and in spite of their resolution greeted him and offered to wash his feet and do all that he might require. It struck awe in their hearts. But they addressed him as Gotama after his family. Then their Lord said to them: "Call me not after my private name, for it is a rude and careless way of addressing one who has obtained Saintship (Arhatship). My mind is undisturbed whether people treat me with respect or disrespect. But it is not courteous for others to call one who looks equally with a kind heart upon all living beings by his familiar name. Buddhas bring salvation to the world, and therefore they ought to be treated with respect as children treat their fathers."

Then he preached to them his first great sermon.

It is known as the "Sermon at Benares," the Dharma-chakra-pravartana Sutra, in which he explained the Four Great

Truths and the Noble Eightfold Path, and made converts of them. Thoroughly versed in highest truth, full of all-embracing intelligence, the Buddha on their account briefly declared to them the one true Way, the Middle Way.

"These are the two extremes, O bhikshus (Religious Wanderers) which the man who has given up the world ought not to follow—the habitual practice, on the one hand, of self-indulgence which is unworthy, vain and fit only for the worldly-minded—and the habitual practice, on the other hand, of self-mortification which is painful, useless and unprofitable.

"Neither abstinence from fish or flesh, nor going naked, nor shaving the head, nor wearing matted hair, nor dressing in a rough garment, nor covering oneself with dirt, nor sacrificing to Fire, will cleanse a man who is not free from delusions.

"Anger, drunkenness, obstinacy, bigotry, deception, envy, self-praise, disparaging others, superciliousness and evil intentions, these constitute uncleanness; not verily the eating of flesh.

"A middle path, O bhikshus, avoiding these two extremes, has been discovered by the Buddha—a path which opens the eyes, and bestows understanding, which leads to peace of mind, to the higher wisdom, to full enlightenment, to Nirvana.

"Scatter the fire amid the desert grass, dried by the sun, fanned by the wind—the raging flames who shall extinguish?

Such is the fire of greediness and lust, I, then, reject both these extremes: my heart keeps in the middle way.

"He who fills his lamp with water will not dispel the darkness, and he who tries to light a fire with rotten wood will fail.

"He in whom self has become extinct is free from lust; the self-indulgent man is led around by his passions, and pleasure-seeking is degrading and vulgar.

"But to satisfy the necessities of life is not evil. To keep the body in good health is a duty, for otherwise we shall not be able to trim the lamp of wisdom, and keep our mind strong and clear."

And then the All-knowing One expounded the joyful news of the truth of suffering and the destruction of that suffering. Amazed were the five mendicants, led by the great Kaundinya, to learn that happiness could only come through recognition of sorrow! And he showed them the Eightfold Path of proper ideas, the torch to light the way; proper aspirations, the guide; proper kind speech, the dwelling-place on the road; proper behavior, and the gait cannot be but straight ahead; proper ways of earning livelihood, so as to harm no living thing or cheat no fellow creature, this the refreshment of the holy man, the good man, the happy man; proper efforts the steps and strides themselves along the path immemorial oft forgot and found again; proper thoughts be breathing, thoughts mindful of the true nature of reality which is like a magic reflection in a dream, a mirage ("In reality it is all a similar emptiness, but you are not free for reality, O my bhikshus?"); and proper meditation the clear adorable peace that follows in the footprints thus implanted in the dust.

This was the message of deliverance, the glad tidings, the sweetness of the truth. "And when the Blessed One had thus set the royal chariot wheel of truth rolling onward, a rapture thrilled through the universes.

"Truly, O Buddha, our Lord, thou hast found the truth!" cried Kaundinya, discerning suddenly with his mental eye, then the other bhikshus too joined him and exclaimed: "Truly, thou art the Buddha, thou hast found the truth."

The five mendicant ascetics received the ordination and formed the first nucleus of the holy brotherhood of disciples known as the Sangha (the Church.) Millions and millions were to come after them. Buddha walked into Benares and begged his meal. Like water that conquers the valleys of the world because it is good at keeping low, Buddha was the conqueror of the world because he chose the lowest role. At the same time this was the most precious of teachings, the Teaching Without Words, teaching humility and charity to the good householders of the land, who, seeing this tall imposing Lord of Men coming meekly to their back doors with a begging pot, learned thereby the childlike and trusting lesson with their very eyes.

Then he went to a tree outside of town, apart from the busy road, ate, put away his bowl, sat down with his legs underneath, and meditated in holy rapture.

There was a youth called Yasa, who was the son of a very wealthy merchant in Benares, who had suddenly become disgusted at the sight of the sleeping women of his harem and was wandering like a madman much distressed by the sorrows of the world. His fifty-four wild buddies were following him across the field, he was so amazing. He came to the Buddha crying: "Alas! What sorrow! What danger!" The Buddha consoled him. As a clean cloth absorbs the dye, Yasa absorbed the teaching that whatsoever is subject to birth is also subject to death. The Buddha pointed out the way to the blessedness of Nirvana, and made him his disciple. Seeing that Yasa had become a bhikshu, his former fifty-four jovial companions also joined the Sangha. The Blessed One sent out these fifty-five new converts and the five original converts as missionaries in different directions to preach his universal religion.

"Go forth, on a journey that shall be for the good of many and for their happiness.

"Go forth in compassion towards the world for the weal of gods and men.

"Go forth in pairs, but each to his own work. Go! rescue and receive.

"Teach the beneficent Law; reveal the holy life to men blinded with the dust of desire.

"They perish for lack of knowledge.

"Teach them the Law."

Thus armed with continence, childlike solitariness, and unwasted vitality they did go out to save the world. The trees were crimson with blossom and the hour big with hope. They would now speak out as Highest Truth what they had always secretly suspected but hitherto with no Edifier such as Buddha to consecrate their certainty. Word had come to them that they were right all along, as in a dream already finished a long time ago. The flower of the Sangha burst out on India and the world. "The fragrance of the righteous travels far and wide."

At this time a man came to Buddha and wanted to know if he couldn't remain at home in a lay position and at the same time reverence the Law. His answer was: "The layman and the hermit are the same, when only both have banished thought of 'self,' looking with equal mind on all that lives."

Shortly afterwards the Buddha had an accession of a thousand new disciples by the conversion of three leading fire-worshipping ascetics, the Kasyapa brothers with all their followers. It was on the Elephant Rock near Gaya with the beautiful valley of Rajagaha stretched out before them, that Buddha, seizing the occasion of a sudden brush fire on the horizon, delivered his famous great Fire Sermon (Aditta-Pariyaya-Sutra) to the thousand assembled fire-sacrificers who had all of them aforetime been monks with matted hair.

"All things, O priests, are on fire. And what, O priests, are all these things which are on fire?

"The eye, O priests, is on fire; forms are on fire; eye-consciousness is on fire; impressions received by the eye are on fire; and whatever sensation, pleasant or unpleasant, or indifferent, originates in dependence on impressions received by the fire, that also is on fire.

"And with what are these on fire?

"With the fire of passions, say I, with the fire of hatred, with the fire of infatuation; with birth, old age, death, sorrow, lamentation, misery, grief, and despair are they on fire.

"The ear is on fire, sounds are on fire; the nose is on fire, odors are on fire; the tongue is on fire, tastes are on fire; the body is on fire, things touchable are on fire; the brain is on fire, ideas are on fire; mind-consciousness is on fire, impressions received by the mind are on fire; and whatever sensation pleasant or unpleasant, or indifferent, originates in dependence on impressions received by the mind, that also is on fire.

"Perceiving this, O priests, the learned and noble being conceives an aversion for the eye, an aversion for forms, an aversion for eye-consciousness, an aversion for impressions received by the eye; and whatever sensation, pleasant or unpleasant, or indifferent, originates in dependence on impressions received by the eye, for that also he conceives an aversion. Conceives an aversion for the ear, sounds; the nose, odors; the tongue, tastes; conceives an aversion for the body, things touchable; for the brain, ideas; for mind-consciousness, for the impressions received by the mind; and whatever sensation, pleasant or unpleasant, or indifferent, originates in dependence on impressions received by the mind, for this also he conceives an aversion.

"And in conceiving this aversion, he becomes divested of passion, and by the absence of passion he becomes free.

"And when he is free, he becomes aware that he is free.

"And he knows that rebirth is exhausted, that he has lived the holy life, that he has done what behooved him to do, and that he is no more for this world."

And that is the reality.

Followed by his numerous disciples the Blessed One descended to Rajagriha the Capital of Magadha.

There, the King Bimbisara, who'd originally questioned the Prince about the advisability of leaving the palace for the homeless life, and then made him promise to return to Rajagriha if he should ever find Perfect Wisdom, came with his advisors, generals, Brahmin priests and merchants to the place where the World-Honored now sat in a quiet grove of trees. When the King and his followers saw the famous Uruvilva Kasyapa with the Blessed One, they wondered what had happened. But Kasyapa made everything clear by prostrating himself at the feet of the Blessed One, and explained how, after seeing the peace of Nirvana, he could no longer find delight in sacrifices and offerings, "which promised no better rewards than pleasures and women," as the old writer states it. For to these ancient monks, clearly perceiving birth as the cause of death, and deeds of lust as the cause of birth, the Buddha was like one standing on the bank calling to the worldly man drifting down the current "Ho there! Wake up! the river in your dream may seem pleasant, but below it is a lake with rapids and crocodiles, the river is evil desire, the lake is the sensual life, its waves are anger, its rapids are lust, and the crocodiles are the women-folk."

The Buddha, studying the person and then teaching the law, perceived that the King and his proud consort were men who had wealth and power but had come to see him because of a considerable doubt that it could do them any good in the end. Truly enlightened, he showed them that there was no individual in the matter of either wealth or poverty, of either enlightenment or ignorance, nay, in either being alive or being dead. He taught them that a man is but a heap of composites.

"After a stronghold has been made of the bones, it is covered with flesh and blood, and there dwell in it old age and death, pride and deceit.

"Look at this dressed up lump, covered with wounds, joined together, sickly full of many a scheme, but which has no strength, no hold.

"There is no room for 'I' and no ground for framing it; so all the accumulated mass of sorrow, sorrows born from life and death, being recognized as attributes of the body, and as this body is not 'I' nor offers ground for 'I,' then comes the great superlative, the source of peace unending.

"The thought of 'self' gives rise to all these sorrows, binding as with cords the world, but having found there is no 'I' that can be bound, then all these bonds are severed.

"There are no bonds indeed—they disappear—and seeing this there is deliverance.

"There is no 'I' at all, in very truth.

"No doer and no knower, no lord, yet notwithstanding this, there ever lasts this birth and death, like morn and night ever recurring.

"But now attend to me and listen: The senses six and their six objects united cause the six kinds of consciousness; the meeting of eye and sight brings forth contact, produces consciousness of sight; the meeting of ear and sound brings forth contact, produces consciousness of sound; the meeting of tongue and taste brings forth contact, produces consciousness of taste; the meeting of nose and odor brings forth contact, produces consciousness of odor; the meeting of body and touchable object brings forth contact, produces consciousness of touch; and the meeting of brain and thought brings forth contact, produces consciousness of thought; then the intervolved effects of recollection follow.

"Then like the burning glass when it is placed over tinder in the high noon sun causes fire to appear, so the sense-organ being placed in contact with the object causes consciousness to appear, and individual self, the parent of consciousness, is born.

"The shoot springs from the seed, the seed is not the shoot, not the shoot and yet not different: such is the birth of all that lives!"

On hearing this discourse on the inconstancy of the self, which, originating from sensation and recollection, must necessarily be subject to the condition of cessation, the King and many of those that accompanied him took refuge in the Three Jewels (Tri-Ratna) of the Buddha, the Dharma, and the Sangha, and became lay followers. The King then invited the Blessed One to the royal palace, entertained him and his bhikshus and presented to the Sangha his pleasure garden, the bamboo grove Veluvana, as a dwelling-place for the homeless disciples of the Great Teacher. He then appointed Jivaka, his renowned physician-in-ordinary, to undertake medical attendance on Buddha and his followers; and it was at the instance of this doctor that the bhikshus, who were previously wearing only cast-off rags, were permitted to accept yellow-dyed robes from pious layfolks.

The bamboo grove was near town but not too close, with many gates and open walks, easy to find for those who sought it, peaceful and quiet all day, mystically silent in the night, far from crowds and roads, a place designed for retreat and undisturbed concentration of the mind on its own pure essence yet charmingly provided with gardens, cloisters, meditation halls, huts, store rooms surrounded by lotus pools, fragrant mango trees and slender fan palms that stood high in the sky like ethereal flowers, like fantastic watery umbrellas of living pain reminding the monks, as they looked, of how seeds, like pleasures, disturbed the balance of the Happy Ground and sprung phantasies of trees sky-high.

One day in Rajagriha one of the first five converts that were ordained by the Buddha, the former ascetic Asvajit, was going on his alms-seeking round with his begging bowl when the monk Sariputra came along and was so struck by Asvajit's appearance of joyfulness and dignity that he asked: "Who is your teacher and what doctrine does he profess?" Sariputra had a spiritual blood-brother named Maudgalyayana; long ago they'd agreed, the first one to find Ambrosia and to know the truth, must tell the other; now as Asvajit spoke, saying, "There is a great sage, a son of the Sakyas, who has gone forth to the homeless life; he is my teacher and it is his doctrine I profess," and sang it in the well-known lines:

"Whatever things proceed from a cause,
Of them the Buddha has stated the cause
And what their dissolution is.
This is what the Great One teaches,"

Sariputra knew at once he had found Ambrosia and went to Maudgalyayana and told him what he had heard. They both attained to the pure eye for the truth and went with all their followers to the Tathagata. On seeing them coming on the road the Blessed One said:

"These two men who come shall be my two most eminent followers, one unsurpassed for wisdom (Maudgalyayana), the other for powers miraculous (Sariputra). Welcome!"

Authorship of various important sections of the Sacred Canon, has now been ascribed to these two brilliant saints. With all their followers they took refuge in the Order.

There was a Brahmin Sage of immense wealth, Mahae Kasyapa, a wise philanthrophic priest whose renown had spread far, who had just renounced his handsome, virtuous wife and all his estate and possessions to find out the way of salvation. Much disturbed, like Yasa the wild boy, he wandered into Buddha's camp in the middle of the night.

"Having rejoiced in the true law, and being humbly desirous for a pure and believing heart, thou hast overcome desire for sleep, and art here to pay me reverence," spoke the Buddha gently. "Now then will I for your sake discharge fully the duties of a first meeting. Famous for your charity, now take from me the charity of perfect rest, and for this end accept my rules of purity."

The All-Knowing One wished to quiet the rich man's contumacious exercise of the distribution of unneeded largesse, to teach him needed rest foremost. "The restless busy nature of the world, this I declare is at the root of pain.

"Seeing the constant toil of birth and death we ought to strive to attain a passive state: the final goal of Sammata, the place of immortality and rest.

"All is empty! neither 'self,' nor place for 'self,' but all the world is like a phantasy; this is the way to regard ourselves, as but a heap of composite qualities."

Mahae Kasyapa understood that there is no "I" in the matter of charity.

"Now you have seen the true doctrine, your guileless heart loves to exercise its charity; for wealth and money are inconstant treasures, 'twere better quickly to bestow such things on others.

"For when a treasure has been burnt, whatever precious things may have escaped the fire the wise man, knowing their inconstancy, gives freely, doing acts of kindness with his saved possessions.

"But the fool guards them carefully, fearing to lose them, worn by anxiety, pestered by imaginary fears in his nightmare that he may lose 'all,' yea, even him-'self.'

"The charitable man suffers no repentance, no torment-ing fear! this is the opening flower of his reward, the fruit that follows—hard to conjecture! This wisdom leads the way to fixed composure without dependence and without numbers.

"Hear!

"And if we even reach the immortal path, still by continuous acts of charity we fulfill ourselves in consequence of kindly char-ity done elsewhere.

"Know then! the charitable man has found the cause of final rescue; even as the man who plants the sapling thereby receives the shade, the flowers, the fruit of the tree fullgrown; the result of charity is even so, its reward is joy and the great Nirvana.

"Giving away our food we get more strength, giving away our clothes we get more beauty; founding religious rest-places we reap the perfect fruit of the highest and the best degree of charity, without self-interest or thought of getting more; and so the heart comes back and rests."

This was the preaching of what was later known as the Dana Paramita, the Ideal of Charity, one of six such ideals fitting into the last six steps of the Eightfold Path like a beautiful ornament. They are the Dana, Ideal of Charity; the Sila, Ideal of Kindness; the Kshanti, Ideal of Patience; the Virya, Ideal of Zeal; the Dhyana, Ideal of Meditation; and the Prajna, Ideal of Wisdom. The great Brahmin, having received this sermon and becoming converted, sang this song:

"Low have I laid the heavy load I bore,
Cause for rebirth is found in me no more.
For never thought for raiment nor for food,
Nor when to rest does the great mind affect
Immeasurable, of our Gotama.
The neck of him is like the fourfold tower
Of mindfulness set up; yea, the great Seer
Has faith and confidence for hands;
Above, the brow of him is insight; nobly wise
He ever walks in cool blessedness."

After the death of Buddha, Mahae Kasyapa became the First Patriarch of the Buddhist Church and organized the all important compilation of the Buddhist Scriptures, the Sacred Canon (the Tripitaka, or, Three Baskets) without which none of the Blessed One's words would have reached us 2,500 years beyond. But in the mind of the Buddha, the Awakened One, these 2,500 years are just a dewdrop. "The line of the law forms an unbroken continuity. In all directions of space are standing Buddhas, like sand of the Ganges: these also do, for the welfare of all beings in the world, expound superior enlightenment. And myself also, am now manifesting, for the welfare of creatures now living, this Buddha-enlightenment by thousands of ten millions of various directions. I reveal the law in its multifariousness and dispositions of creatures. I use different means to rouse each according to his own character. Therefore try to understand the mystery of the Buddhas, the holy Masters of the world; forsake all doubt and uncertainty: you shall become Buddhas: rejoice!"

After the conversion of Mahae Kasyapa, walking in the path of earth Gotama Sakyamuni returned to the country where he was born, Gorakpur District, where his father King Suddhodhana reigned. Followed by his numerous Men of Saintship, yet advancing with the grave mysterious loneliness of the elephant, he came to within several miles of Kapilavastu where the sumptuous palace of his youth still stood, as unreal now, in his enlightened mirror-like reflection, as an indicated castle in a child's tale designed solely to make children believe in its existence. The King heard of his arrival and came at once, eagerly concerned.

On seeing him he uttered these mournful words: "Thus, now I see my son, his well known features as of old; but how estranged his heart! There are no grateful outflowings of soul; cold and vacant there he sits."

They looked at each other like people thinking upon a distant friend gazing by accident upon his pictured form.

Buddha: "I know that the King's heart is full of love and recollection, and that for his son's sake he adds to grief further grief; but now let the bands of love that bind him, thinking of his son, be instantly unloosed and utterly destroyed.

"Ceasing from thoughts of love, let your calmed mind receive from me, your son, religious nourishment such as no son has offered yet to father; such do I present to you the King, my father.

"The way superlative of bliss immortal I offer now the Maharajah; from the accumulating of deeds comes birth; as the result of deeds comes the recompense. Knowing then that deeds bring fruit, as the wheel follows the foot of the ox that draws the carriage, how diligently should you be to rid yourself of worldly deeds! how careful that in the world your deeds should be only good and gentle!

"But not for the sake of a heavenly birth should you practice gentle deeds but that by day and night, rightly free from thoughts unkind, loving all that lives and equally, you may strive to get rid of all confusion of the mind and practice silent con-templation; only this brings profit in the end, beside this there is no reality.

"For be sure! earth, heaven, and hell are as but froth and bubble of the sea.

"Nirvana! This is the chief rest.

"Composure! that the best of all enjoyments.

"Infinitely quiet is the place where the wise man finds his abode; no need of arms or weapons there! no elephants or horses, chariots or soldiers there!

"Banished, once for all, birth, age, and death.

"Subdued the power of greedy desire and angry thoughts and ignorance, there's nothing left in the wide world to conquer!"

Having heard from his son how to cast off fear and escape the evil ways of birth, and in a manner of such dignity and tenderness, the King himself left his kingly estate and country and entered on the calm flowings of thoughts, the gate of the true law of eternality. Sweet in meditation, dew Suddhodana drank. In the night, recalling his son with pride, he looked up at the infinite stars and suddenly realized "How glad I am to be alive to reverence this starry universe!" then "But it's not a case of being alive and the starry universe is not necessarily the starry universe" and he realized the utter strangeness and yet commonness of the unsurpassable wisdom of the Buddha.

Accompanied by Maudgalyayana, the Blessed One visited the woman who had been his wife, the Princess Yasodhara in the Palace, for the purpose of taking his son Rahula on the road with him. Princess Yasodhara pleaded for the inheritance of the boy, who was now nineteen years old. "I will give him a more excellent inheritance," said Buddha, and bade Maudgalyayana shave his head, and admit him to the Sangha Brotherhood.

After this they started out from Kapilavistu. In the pleasure gardens they came upon a party of Sakya princes, all cousins of Gotama, among them his cousins Ananda and Devadatta, who were to become, respectively, his greatest friend and his greatest enemy. Some years later when the Blessed One inquired of Ananda what it was that had impressed him in the Buddha's way of life and most influenced him to forsake all worldly pleasures and enabled him to cut asunder his youthful sexual cravings so as to realize the true Essence of Mind and its self-purifying brightness, Ananda joyfully replied: "Oh, my Lord! the first thing that impressed me were the thirty-two marks of excellency in my Lord's personality. They appeared to me so fine, as tender and brilliant, and transparent as a crystal." This warm-hearted youth ranked but next to Maudgalyayana in brilliance of learning, but it was this combination of near-infatuated love for the Master and the superior erudite sharpness that prevented him from attaining to the states of equal-minded bliss experienced by the least of the bhikshus, some of them uneducated antiquity hoboes like Sunita the Scavenger, Alavaka the Cannibal (he had been an actual cannibal in Atavi prior to his enlightenment), or Ugrasena the Acrobat. Ananda became known as the Shadow, ever following the Blessed One's footsteps, even when he paced, step for step and right behind, turning where he turned, sitting when he sat. After awhile it became habit for Ananda to serve his Master, such as preparing his sitting place, or going ahead to make arrangements in towns, providing him with little kindnesses when needed, constantly a companion and personal attendant, which the Blessed One accepted quietly.

In grievous contrast was the other cousin Devadatta. Jealous and foolish he joined the Order hoping to learn the Transcendental Samapatti graces that come after highest holy meditation so he could use them as powerful magic, even against the Buddha, if necessary, in his plans to found a new sect of his own. The Samapatti graces included Transcendental Telepathy. Devadatta's evil avarice was not apparent in that first meeting in the gardens of Gorakpur. Looking upon all beings as equally to be loved, equally empty, and equally coming Buddhas it made little difference to the Blessed One what Devadatta harbored in his heart in the moment of ordination. Even later after Devadatta had made attempts on his life, as will be shown, with mighty sweetness the Exalted One blessed his inner heart.

The Teacher and his disciples moved on to Rajagaha where they were greeted by the immensely wealthy merchant Sudatta, who was called Anathapindika on account of his charities to the orphans and the poor. This man had just bought at an enormous price the magnificent Jetavana Park from a royal prince and built a splendid monastery of eighty cells and other residences with terraces and baths for the Buddha and his ordained disciples. The Blessed One accepted his invitation and made his abode there, right outside the great city of Sravasti. During the rainy seasons he came back to Rajagaha to stay in the monastery of the Bamboo Grove.

Most of the time he spent in solitude in the forest; the other monks sat apart, also practicing meditation, drinking in the example of the tremendous love-filled silence that emanated from the part of the forest where the Buddha sat meek on a throne of grass, long-suffering beneath the patience of the tree that sheltered him. Sometimes this life was pleasant ("Forests are delightful; where the world finds no delight, there the passionless will find delight, for they look not for pleasures"); sometimes it was not pleasant:

"Cold, master, is the winter night," sang the monks. "The time of frost is coming; rough is the ground with the treading of the hoofs of cattle; thin is the couch of leaves, and light is the yellow robe: the winter wind blows keen." But these men had roused and awakened themselves, as their forefather saints in the long tradition of the Indias, to the incomparable dignity of knowing that there are worse things than the stinging fly, the creeping snake, winter's cold rain or summer's scorching wind. Having escaped the grief of lust, and dissipated the clouds and mists of sensual desire, Buddha accepted food both good or bad, whatever came, from rich or poor, without distinction, and having filled his alms-dish, he then returned back to the solitude, where he meditated his prayer for the emancipation of the world from its bestial grief and incessant bloody deeds of death and birth, death and birth, the ignorant gnashing screaming wars, the murder of dogs, the histories, follies, parent beating child, child tormenting child, lover ruining lover, robber raiding niggard, leering, cocky, crazy, wild, blood-louts moaning for more blood-lust, utter sots, running up and down simpleminded among charnels of their own making, simpering everywhere, mere tsorises and dream-pops, one monstrous beast raining forms from a central glut, all buried in unfathomable darkness crowing for rosy hope that can only be complete extinction, at base innocent and without any vestige of self-nature whatever; for should the causes and conditions of the ignorant insanity of the world be removed, the nature of its non-insane non-ignorance would be revealed, like the child of dawn entering heaven through the morning in the lake of the mind, the Pure,

True Mind, the source, Original Perfect Essence, the empty void radiance, divine by nature, the sole reality, Immaculate, Universal, Eternal, One Hundred Percent Mental, upon which all this dreamfilled darkness is imprinted, upon which these unreal bodying forms appear for what seems to be a moment and then disappear for what seems to be eternity.

Thousands of monks followed the Awakened One, and beat a track behind his path. On the last autumnal plain full-moon night the Exalted One took his seat in the midst of the assembly of monks under the canopy of heaven. And the Exalted One beheld the silent, calm assembly of monks and spoke to them as follows:

"Not a word is spoken, O Monks, by this assembly, not a word is uttered, O Monks, by this assembly, this assembly consists of pure kernel.

"Such is, O Monks, this fraternity of disciples, that it is worthy of offerings, of oblations, of gifts and homage and is the noblest community in the world.

"Such is, O Monks, this fraternity of disciples, that a small gift given to it becomes great, and a great gift given to it becomes greater still.

"Such is, O Monks, this fraternity of disciples, that it is difficult to find one like it in the world.

"Such is, O Monks, this fraternity of disciples, that one is glad to walk many miles to behold it, and even if it be only from behind.

"Such is, O Monks, this fraternity of disciples, such is, O Monks, this assembly, that, O Monks, there are among these disciples some monks who are Perfect Ones, who have reached the end of all illusion, who have arrived at the goal, who have accomplished the task, have cast off the burden, have won their deliverance, who have destroyed the fetters of existence, and who, through superior knowledge, have liberated themselves."

And to the Awakened One who had come before him and to all Buddhas in all times throughout the universes he prayed the Heart of the Great Dharani, the center of his crowning Prayer, for the emancipation of the world from its incessant birth and dying:

"Om! O thou who holdest the seal of power
Raise thy diamond hand,
Bring to naught,
Destroy,
Exterminate.
O thou sustainer,
Sustain all who are in extremity.
O thou purifier,
Purify all who are in bondage to self.

May the ender of suffering be victorious.
O thou perfectly enlightened,
Enlighten all sentient beings.
O thou who art perfect in wisdom and compassion
Emancipate all beings
And bring them to Buddhahood, amen."

As the Word of awakening spread around, the ladies cut off their hair, put on the yellow robe, took begging bowls, and came out to meet Buddha. No, he said, "As water is held up by a strong dyke, so have I established a barrier of regulations which are not to be transgressed." But since even the Princess Yasodhara and his devoted maternal aunt Prajapati Gotami were among this elite group of earnest and fearless women, and Ananda with typical affectionateness and at the importunate insistence of Gotama's aunt interceded so fervently in their favor, the Blessed One relented and the Sisterhood of Bhikshunis came into being. "Let them be subject and subordinate to the brethren," he commanded.

"Even so," spoke the Holy One, "their admission means that the Good Law shall not endure for a thousand years, but only for five hundred. For as when mildew falls upon a field of rice that field is doomed, even so when women leave the household life and join an Order, that Order will not long endure."

Coupled with this was his premonition of the troubles that came in after days when Devadatta rose up and used some of the nuns for his schemes.

The Great King Prasenajit, whose kingdom dwelt in mighty peace yet himself being beset with confusion and doubt after a falling-out with his erstwhile beloved queen, and wishing at this time to hear the good and evil law from the lips of the Honored of the Worlds, found the Buddha, approached him respectfully from the right side, paid his compliments, and sat down.

To King Prasenajit the Tiger of the Law said: "Even those who, by evil Karma, have been born in low degree, when they see a person of virtuous character feel reverence for him; how much rather ought an independent king, who by his previous conditons of life has acquired much merit, when he encounters Buddha, to conceive even more reverence.

"Nor is it difficult that a country should enjoy more rest and peace, by the presence of Buddha, than if he were not to dwell therein.

"Now then, for the sake of the great ruler, I will briefly relate the good and evil law. The great requirement is a loving heart! To regard the people as we do an only son; not to exercise one's self in false theories, nor to ponder much on kingly dignity, nor to listen to the smooth words of false teachers.

"Not to vex one's self by 'lying on a bed of nails,' but to

meditate deeply on the vanity of earthly things, to realize the fickleness of life by constant recollection.

"Not to exalt one's self by despising others, but to retain an inward sense of happiness resulting from one's self, and to look forward to increased happiness hereafter resulting also from one's own self.

"Hear, O Maharajah! Self be your lantern, self be your refuge, no other refuge! The Established Law be your lantern, the Established Law be your refuge!

"Evil words will be repeated far and wide by the multitude, but there are few to follow good direction.

"As when enclosed in a fourstone mountain, there is no escape or place of refuge for anyone, so within this sorrow-piled mountain-wall of old age, birth, disease, and death, there is no other escape for the world than the practicing of the true law by one's own self.

"All the ancient conquering kings, who were as gods on earth, thought by their strength to overcome decay; but after a brief life they too disappeared.

"Look at your royal chariot; even it is showing signs of wear and tear.

"The Aeon-fire will melt Mount Sumeru, the great water of the ocean will be dried up, how much less can our human frame, which is as a bubble and a thing of unreality, kept through the suffering of the long night of life pampered by wealth, living idly and in carelessness, how does this body expect to endure for long upon the earth! Death suddenly comes and it is carried away as rotten wood in a stream.

"Thick mists nurture the place of moisture, the fierce wind scatters the thick mists, the sun's rays encircle Mount Sumeru, the fierce fire licks up the place of moisture, so things are ever born once more to be destroyed.

"The Being who is Cooled, not lagging on the road of the law, expecting these changes, frees himself from engagements, he is not occupied with self-pleasing, he is not entangled by any of the cares of life, he holds to no business, seeks no friendships, engages in no learned career, nor yet wholly separates himself from it; for his learning is the wisdom of not-perceiving wisdom, but yet perceiving that which tells him of his own momentariness.

"The wise ones know that, though one should be born in heaven, there is yet no escape from the changes of time and the changes of self, the pernicious rules of existence even heavenly; their learning, then, is to attain to the changeless mind; for where no change is, there is peace.

"The changeless body of life immortal is offered all; it is the mind-magic-body (manomayakaya); all beings are coming Buddhas because all beings are coming no-bodies; and all beings were past Buddhas because all beings were past no-bodies; and thus, in truth, all beings are already Buddhas because all beings are already no-bodies.

"For the possession of changeful body is the foundation of all pain.

"Conceive a heart, loathe lust; put away this condition, receive no more sorrow. For lust is change, lust is desires unequally yoked like two staggering oxen, lust is loss of love.

"When a tree is burning with fierce flames how can the little sister-birds congregate therein?

"The wise man, who is regarded as an enlightened sage, without this knowledge is ignorant.

"To neglect this knowledge is the mistake of life.

"All the teaching of the schools should be centered here; without it is no true reason."

Hearing these words King Prasenajit went back home and reconciled with his queen. He became quiet and joyful. He had learned that the want of faith is the engulfing sea of ignorance, the presence of disorderly belief is the rolling flood of lust; but wisdom is the handy boat, reflection is the hold-fast by which to win access to the other shore and find eternal safety. But King Prasenajit was not yet enlightened nor wholly a believer in the Buddha, for in his joy and religious enthusiasm he now ordered sacrificial rites in order to obtain merit beyond the merit of the sermon.

The Blessed One was at Sravasti, in the Jeta grove in Anathapindika's park. A number of monks having risen early and dressed and taken bowl and robe, entered Sravasti for alms. After their return they sought the presence of Buddha and told him of the preparations for a great sacrifice being arranged to be held for King Prasenajit. Five hundred bulls, five hundred bullocks, and as many heifers, goats, and round-horned rams were led to the pillar to be sacrificed, after which the slaves and menials and craftsmen, hectored about by blows and by fear, made the preparations with tearful faces weeping. Hearing of this evil murderousness, the Exalted One understood as ever that men were shamed and debased forever, and only because of ignorance.

"To slaughter the gentle lamblike beast that fills your pail with milk, for to eat of its suffering flesh, is evil and sin, foolish the hand that holds the knife in the general emptiness, bound to haunt the butcher to his sop's successive graves; but O my bhikshus, brothers, how much more evil, more sin still, to take the kindly ox and other beasts, hapless are their eyes, and swill them in drunken hacking bloodbath sacrifice for the sake of gaining one's own rebirth yet again in heavens of self and pain.

"Whatever a man sacrifice in this world as an offering or as an obligation for a whole year in order to gain merit, the whole of it is not worth a quarter of a centavo.

"All creatures tremble at punishment, all creatures love life; remember that thou art like unto them, and do not kill, nor cause slaughter.

"He, seeking his own happiness, that punishes or kills creatures who also long for happiness, will not find happiness after death.

"A man is not religious because he injures living creatures; because he has pity on all living creatures, therefore is a man called religious.

"In seeking to escape from suffering ourselves, why should we inflict it upon others?

"Unless you can so control your minds that even the thought of brutal unkindness and killing is abhorrent, you will never be able to escape from the bondage of suffering.

"Pure and earnest monks and Wise Beings, when walking a narrow path, will never so much as tread on the growing grass beside the path.

"It is only such true and sincere bhikshus who have repaid their Karmic debts of previous lives, who will attain true emancipation, and who will no more be bound to wander to this triple world of sense, contact, and suffering.

"How can a religious man, who hopes to become a deliverer of others, himself be living or gaining afterlife on the flesh of other sentient beings?

"So all dedicated men must be careful to live in all sincerity, refraining from even the appearance of unkindness to other life."

Hearing of these words, learning that the Buddha regarded sacrifice as so much rueful butchery, the King returned, came into the presence of the Holy One, and after exchanging greetings with him and compliments of friendship and courtesy, sat down at one side. So seated he said to the Holy One:

"Does Master Gotama also make no claim to be perfectly and supremely enlightened?"

"If there be anyone, sire, to whom such enlightenment might rightly be attributed, it is I. I verily, sire, am perfectly and supremely enlightened."

"But Master Gotama, there are recluses and Brahmins who also, like yourself, have each their order of disciples, their attendant followers, who are teachers of disciples, well-known and reputed theorizers, highly esteemed by the people. Now they, when I've asked this same question of them, have not laid claim to perfect and supreme enlightenment. How can this be? For Master Gotama is young in years, and is a novice in the life of religion."

"There are four young creatures who are not to be disregarded or despised because they are youthful," replied the Buddha. "What are the four?

"A noble prince.

"A snake.

"A fire.

"A monk.

"Yea, sire, these four young creatures are not to be disregarded or despised because they are youthful."

When these things had been said, King Prasenajit spoke thus to the Exalted One: "Most excellent, Lord, most excellent! Just as if a man were to set up that which has been thrown down, or were to reveal that which is hidden away, or were to point out the right road to him who has gotten lost, or were to bring a lamp into the darkness, so that those who have eyes could see external forms—even so, Lord, has the truth been made known to me in many a figure by the Exalted One. I, even I, Lord, betake myself to the Exalted One as my refuge to the Established Law and to the Order. May the Exalted One accept me as a follower, as one who from this day and forth as long as life endures has taken his refuge therein."

And this King kept his word, and aged with the Buddha himself throughout the rest of their natural lives.

The manner in which the Enlightened One ordinarily spent each day was very simple. Rising at dawn he would wash and dress himself without assistance. He would then meditate in solitude till it was time to go on his round for the daily meal without which he could not go on living and practicing the Dharma. When the time arrived, dressing himself suitably, with his bowl in his hand, alone or attended by some disciples, he would visit the neighboring town or village. After finishing his meal in some house, he would discourse on the Dharma to the host and his family with due regard to their capacity for spiritual enlightenment, return to his seating-mat or depending on the rainy season his lodgings and wait till all his followers had finished their meal. He would discourse to the monks and suggest subjects for thought or give them exercises in meditation suited to their attainments or else finally remind them that the stopping of all thoughts and all conceptions, the curing the mind of thoughts and of the very thought of thoughts, is the practice that leads to Nirvana. They would then leave him, going off each to his own favorite spot to meditate. During the heat of the Indian day he would lie down and take a short rest, lying down on his right side in the lion posture with knee on knee and head on hand, in the traditional posture he recommended for sleep and for which reason he was sometimes called The Lion of the Sakyas; but in this midday repose he would not sleep, nor practice a systematic meditation, rather he would simply rest and ponder rest.

In the afternoon he would meet the folks from the neighboring villages or towns assembled in the lecture-hall, or in the shady grove of trees, take pity on them and advise and discourse to them according to their individual needs and thought-capacities. In this connection, for instance, when the woman Visakha sat on one side crying during one of these gatherings, because she could not bear the loss of her granddaughter who'd just died, the Blessed One asked her how many men were living in Sravasti.

"Lord, men say there are seven times ten millions."

"If all these were like thy granddaughter, wouldst thou not love them?"

"Verily, Lord."

"And how many die daily in Sravasti?"

"Many, Lord."

"Then there is never a moment when thou wouldst not be grieving for someone!"

"True, Master."

"Wouldst thou then spend thy life weeping day and night?"

"I understand, Lord; it is well said!"

"Grieve then no more."

At the close of the day, after refreshing himself with a bath when necessary, the Buddha would explain difficulties to expound the doctrine to some of his disciples, showing them the psychological techniques suitable for making all kinds of people with all their differently hindered, wounded mentalities understand the single vehicle of the Law as made multifariously manifest. "Buddhas while manifesting skillfulness display various vehicles through, at the same time indicating the single Buddha-vehicle, the supreme place of blessed rest.

"Acquainted as they are with the conduct of all mortals, with their peculiar dispositions and previous actions, the Buddhas, using different means to rouse each according to his own character, impart their lights to them.

"Such is the might of their knowledge."

Thus spending the first watch of the night in teaching and sometimes in discourse with other monks on the occasions when he would walk into their midst from the outer night demanding "What are you talking about now, O monks, what has risen to trouble you now, O monks?" he would spend the rest of the evening pacing up and down in front of his spot or his open verandah, meditating, shadowed by Ananda who paced ever behind him.

"If a man hold himself dear, let him watch himself carefully; during one at least out of the three watches a wise man should be watchful."

Then he would sleep.

"Sitting alone, lying down alone, walking alone without ceasing, and alone subduing himself, let a man be happy near the edge of a forest," is the saying in the Dhammapada, the Footsteps of the Law.

"Well-makers lead the water wherever they like;
fletchers bend the arrow; carpenters bend a log
of wood, good people fashion themselves."
                              —DHAMMAPADA

One day Ananda asked the Blessed One for advice about how to comport oneself in the presence of women.

"Avoid them altogether, Ananda."

"But supposing they approach us, Blessed Lord?"

"Speak not to them, Ananda."

"But supposing they ask us a question, Blessed Lord?"

"Then keep wide awake, Ananda."

And the Holy One said: "When, however, you must speak to women, consider them, if they are aged, as mothers, and if they are young, treat them as sisters."

It came to pass that a certain Lady Amra, a beautiful courtesan who had received great sums of money from wealthy merchants of Vaisali, conceived in her mind the idea of offering her stately mansion and mango grove to the Master and the Brotherhood. She was graceful, pleasant, gifted with the complexion of a young rose, well-versed in dancing, singing and lute-playing; now, despite her possession of these highest feminine prizes, she wished to offer her life to the religious law. She sent a message to the Blessed One offering the mansion and the gardens for the convenience of his followers, and he accepted graciously.

Seated in the mango grove one day, he received another message from the Lady Amra requesting an audience, to which he acceded.

"This woman," he told the assembled followers as she was seen coming down the garden with her servants, "is indeed exceedingly beautiful, able to fascinate the minds of the religious; now then, keep your recollection straight! Let wisdom keep your mind in subjection!

"Better to fall into the fierce tiger's mouth, or under the sharp knife of the executioner, than to dwell with a woman and excite in yourselves lustful thoughts, and thus become entangled in her net of plans, which is birth, the trap for death.

"A woman is anxious to exhibit her form and shape, whether walking, standing, sitting, or sleeping.

"Men being men are not free from their offices of lust, action bestowed by the Karma of previous cupidities and concupiscent thoughts; women being women are the innocent vessels of human rebirth incarnadined and personified, man's own flesh-handful of lust; mutually attracted, mutually victimized by their Karmas, mutually made and then removed by their Karmas, with no 'I' to say Nay in the matter, men and women roll the wheel of death along for the sake of frottings, pride, and happiness.

"But what kind of happiness is this, straining in the emptiness to gratify the ungratifyable senses! There is no gratifying, no appeasing the wild heart! Your loins be rent and there is no gratifying it.

"The cup of life is a bottomless horror, like drinking and drinking in a dream to slake a thirst beyond reason and unreal.

"Look at the empty sky!—how may he grab greedy fistfuls of it, cupiditous man? How may he hack and kill the unkillable, that benumbed and haunted dreamer?

"All is empty everywhere forever, wake up! The mind is fool and limited, to take these senses, petty thwartings in a dream, as reality; as if the deeps of the ocean were moved by the wind that ripples the waves. And that wind is ignorance.

"A woman wants to give rebirth, it is in her Karma to be afraid of being barren and alone, yet the world has no more reality than if you were to say, 'It is a barren woman's child.'

"Even when represented as a picture, a woman desires most of all to set off the blandishments of her beauty, and thus to rob men of their steadfast heart.

"How then ought you to guard yourselves? By regarding her tears and her smiles as enemies, her stooping form, her hanging arms, and all her disentangled hair as toils designed to entrap man's heart.

"Then how much more should you suspect her studied,

amorous beauty; when she displays her dainty outline, her richly ornamented form, and chatters gayly with the foolish man!

"Ah, then, what perturbation and what evil thoughts, not seeing underneath the horrid, tainted shape, the sorrows of impermanence, the impurity, the unreality!

"Considering these as the reality, all lustful thoughts die out.

"Rightly considering these, within their several limits, not even a heavenly nymph would give you joy.

"But yet the power of lust is great with men, and is to be feared withal, take then the bow of earnest perseverance, and the sharp arrow points of wisdom, cover your head with the helmet of right-thought, and fight with fixed resolve against the five desires.

"Better far with red-hot iron pins bore out both your eyes, than encourage in yourselves lustful thoughts, or look upon a woman's form with such desires.

"Lust beclouding a man's heart, confused with woman's beauty because of the maleness in his Karma, his mind is dazed; and at the end of his life, having demeaned himself with women for a few sexual feelings, evilly involved in the snare of mutual agreement which is her chief delight, that man must fall into an evil way.

"His life spent in house and home, a hole-and-corner life at best, he comes to senility jabbering multitudes of runes, religious in regret.

"Fear then the sorrow of that evil way! Fear then, and harbor not the deceits of the women!

"Let no holy man be cause of further rebirth; for as twelve equals a dozen so birth equals death.

"Refrain from looking at her form; straighten out your thoughts.

"Suppose that there is a maiden of the warrior or of the brahmin or of the householder class, in all the charm of her fifteen or sixteen summers; not too tall, not too short, not too slim, not too stout, not too dark, not too fair—is she not at this period at her very loveliest in form and feature? Whatsoever pleasure and satisfaction arises at the sight of this beauty and loveliness—that is of the delights of form.

"Suppose that, after a time, one sees this same innocent sister when she is eighty or ninety or a hundred years old, broken-down, crooked as a rooftree rafter, bowed, tottering along leaning on a stave, wasted, withered, all wrinkled and blotched, with broken teeth, grey hair, trembling head. What think you, monks? That former loveliness of form and feature—has it not disappeared and given place to wretchedness?

"Again, should one see this sister, sick, suffering, sore afflicted, lying fouled in her own filth, lifted up by others, tended by others—what think you, monks? Is not that which aforetime was beauty and loveliness wholly departed and in its place, wretchedness?

"Again, should one see this sister after the body has been lying at the burial place one, two, or three days, bloated, discolored, putrefying, picked at by crows and hawks, and vultures, gnawed by dogs and jackals, and all manner of crawling things. Or should one see the body, when it is a mere blood-bespattered skeleton, hung with rags of flesh, or when the bones are all scattered this way and that; or when, white as a sea shell, they are flung together in a heap, or when, after the lapse of a year, they are all weathered away to dust.

"What think you, monks?

"All that grace and beauty which was aforetime—is it not wholly fled, and in its place, wretchedness?

"But this is the wretchedness of form."

The Lady Amra, clothed to fit the occasion so that her charm was not set off to excite, but simply covered, her thoughts at rest, suffered there to be made offerings of food and refreshment to the Blessed One and his retinue of tranquil men.

The Buddha addressed her. "Your heart, O lady! seems composed and quiet, your form without external ornaments; young in years and rich, you seem well-talented as you are beautiful.

"That one, so gifted, should by faith be able to receive the law of righteousness is, indeed, a rare thing in the world.

"The wisdom of a master derived from former births, enables him to accept the law with joy; this is not rare. But that a woman, weak of will, scant in wisdom, deeply immersed in love, should yet be able to delight in piety, this, indeed, is very rare.

"A man born in the world, by proper thought comes to delight in the solitude of goodness, he recognizes the impermanence of wealth and beauty, and looks upon religion as his best ornament.

"He feels that this alone can remedy the ills of life and change the fate of young and old; the evil destiny that cramps another's life cannot affect him, living righteously.

"Relying on external help, he has sorrow; self-reliant, there is strength and joy.

"But in the case of woman, from another comes the labor, and the nurture of another's child. Thus then should everyone consider well, and loathe and put away the form of woman."

Lady Amra replied:- "Oh! may the lord, in deep compassion, receive from me, though ignorant, this offering, and so fulfill my earnest vow." And she joined the Sisterhood of Bhikshunis.

From Vaisali the Blessed One went to Sravasti.

It was there in the Jetavana Meditation Hall that the Buddha delivered a discourse to twelve hundred Great Disciples which became known as the <u>Surangama Sutra</u>. It was a high teaching that solved many mental puzzles and succeeded in ridding the greatly intelligent monks of the troublesome doubts which they occasionally experienced in their meditations. Upon hearing this Great Sutra which the Blessed One interpreted with great care, many novice disciples became fully accomplished saints and entered immediately into the Ocean Of Omniscience, for it was the perfect teaching of the practices and attainments of the Tathagata's Secret Path.

An unusual incident had occured that same day, involving Ananda, that served as an impetus to start the discussion. King Prasenajit earlier that day had invited Buddha and his chief Bodhisattva-Mahasattvas (Great Wise Beings) to a special feast at the royal palace. All the other monks young and old had been invited to another feast, so that Ananda, returning to the Jetavana Monastery from a journey to a distant district found no one around and consequently went alone into Sravasti for the begging of his daily meal. While begging from door to door in his neat yellow robe the pretty daughter of a prostitute took a liking to him and implored her mother to work some trick to induce the youthful and attractive monk to come into her room. Ananda being Ananda, warm and impressionable, he soon found himself in Pchiti's room under the influence of the maiden's beauty and the magic spell known as <u>bramanyika</u> as invoked by the mother.

Buddha, returning to the Meditation Hall and settling down with all his disciples for the continuation of the Summer Devotion and the Uposatha public confessions made by the various monks, knew all along where Ananda was and what was happening. Accordingly he sent his "other Ananda," his other constant companion, the Great Bodhisattva of Intellectual Radiance, Manjusri, to the house of the prostitute to recite the Great Dharani (the Great Prayer) so that Ananda would not yield to temptation. As soon as Manjusri complied with his Lord's wishes Ananda returned to self-control and saw that he was dreaming. Manjusri then encouraged both Ananda and Pchiti and they returned with him to the Buddha at the Meditation Hall.

When Ananda came into the presence of Buddha, he bowed down to the ground in great humility, blaming himself that he had not yet fully developed the potentialities of Enlightenment, and had therefore failed to lift the curtain of mortal limitations from his true and original, shining mind, because from the beginning of his previous lives he had too much devoted himself to study and learning of words and ideas. So his mind not being concentrated on its pure essence of perfect patience and undisturbed tranquillity, the universal deep ocean of bliss, he had not been able to resist the lure of the maiden Pchiti or control his own mind and his own body and had reached for external conditions thus abandoning the bright holiness of bhikshuhood for the vain inflammations of animality that belong to the ever returning cycle of deaths and rebirths. Ananda earnestly pleaded with the Buddha and prayed to all the other Tathagatas from the ten quarters of the universe, to support him in attaining perfect Enlightenment, that is, to support him by some most fundamental and expedient means in his practice of the Three Excellencies of Dhyana (Meditation), Samadhi (ecstasy in meditation), and Samapatti (transcendental powers arising from ecstasy in meditation).

At the same time all those in the assembly with one accord and with gleeness of heart, prepared to listen to the instruction to be given to Ananda by the Buddha. With one accord they paid homage to their Lord and then resuming their seats waited in perfect quietness and patience to receive the Sacred Teaching.

The Buddha said: "Ananda! And all of you in this great Dharma assembly! You ought to know and appreciate that the reason why sentient beings by their previous lives since beginningless time have formed a succession of deaths and rebirths, life after life, is because they have never realized the true Essence of Mind and its self-purifying brightness.

"On the contrary, they have been absorbed all the time busying themselves with their deluding and transient thoughts which are nothing but falsity and vanity. Hence they have prepared for themselves the conditions for this ever returning cycle of deaths and rebirths.

"They should keep themselves one with the Tathagatas, who have ever remained, from beginningless time to endless time, of one pure Suchness, undisturbed by any complexity within their minds nor any rising thoughts of discrimination of this or that or the other.

"Ananda, I want to question you; please listen carefully. You once said that at the time your faith in me was awakened, that it was due to seeing the Thirty Two marks of traditional excellence.

"Let me ask you: What was it that gave you the sensation of seeing? And what was it that experienced this? And who was it that was pleased?"

Ananda replied: "At the time I experienced the sensation of being pleased it was both through my eyes and my mind. When my eyes saw, my mind immediately experienced a feeling of being pleased."

The Buddha said: "From what you have just said, Ananda, your feeling of being pleased originated in your eyes yet also in your mind. Ananda, if you do not know where lies the perception of sight and where the activities of the mind originate, you will never be able to subjugate your worldly attachments and contaminations.

"Ananda! if you do not know where the place of origination of your own perception of sight is, it is like a king whose city was pestered by robbers and who tried to put an end to the thieving but was unsuccessful because he could not locate the secret hidingplace of the robbers. So you wander about ignorantly and uncontrolled.

"Let me ask you? Referring to your eyes and mind, do you know their secret hidingplace?"

Ananda replied: "Noble Lord! In all the ten different orders of life, the eyes are in front of the face and the mind is hidden within the body."

The Buddha interrupted: "What is it you first see, as you sit here in the hall looking out the open door?"

Ananda: "First I see my Lord and then the distinguished audience, and only afterwards do I see the trees and the park outside."

Buddha: "What is it that enables you, while looking outside, to distinguish these different sights that your eyes see?"

Ananda: "It is because the door of the hall is wide open."

Buddha: "If your perception of sight really were located within your body, in the same way you would be able to see the inside of your body first, and only afterwards the sights outside, as we do in the hall. But there are no sentient beings who can see both the inside and outside of their bodies."

Ananda, bowing, said: "My mind must be like a lamp, then, a lamp outside my body illuminating the outside sights but not the inside of my body."

Buddha: "If so, how could your mind perceive what your body feels? For instance, as you look at the sights, it's plain that the eyeballs that belong to your body and the perception that belongs to your mind are in perfect mutual cooperation, so what you've just said about the mind existing outside the body is impossible."

Ananda: "But my Lord, it seems that the perceiving mind must be in some locality!"

Buddha: "But Ananda where is its abiding place?"

Ananda: "My perceiving mind must be like a crystal bowl covering my eyes."

Buddha: "If so, perception being lodged in your perceiving mind, you would be able to see your own eyes without the aid of a mirror."

Ananda: "Lord, it must be that my perceiving mind must be abiding between my eyes and the objects of sight that I see."

Buddha: "Ananda, now you think that the Mind must be abiding between somethings. How can the perceiving mind be abiding between the location of the eyes and the location of the sight-objects, when the perceiving mind and the eye are as one in perfect mutual cooperation?"

Ananda: "Some time ago when my Lord was discussing the intrinsic Dharma with the four great Wise Beings Maudgalya-yana, Subhuti, Purna, and Sariputra, I overheard my Lord to say, that the essence of the discerning, perceiving conscious mind existed neither inside nor outside, nor between, in fact, that it had no location of existence."

Buddha: "Ananda, the essence of the discerning, perceptive, conscious mind has no definite location anywhere; it is neither in this world, in the vast open spaces, neither in water, nor on land, neither flying with wings, nor walking, nor is it any-where."

Thereupon Ananda rose from his place in the midst of the assembly, adjusted his ceremonial scarf, knelt upon his right knee, placed the palms of his hands together, and respectfully addressed the Buddha, saying: "My Noble Lord! In spite of all I have gained mentally, I have not become liberated from con-taminations and attachments and consequently I could not over-come the magic spell at the home of a harlot. My mind became confused and I was at the point of drowning in its defilement. I can see now that it was wholly due to my ignorance as to the right realization of what is true and essential Mind. I pray thee, O my Lord, to have pity and mercy upon me and show me the right Path to the spiritual graces that come with ecstasy in med-itation, so that I may attain to self-mastery and become emancipated from the lure of evil and the sufferings of successive deaths and rebirths."

Then the Buddha addressed the assembly, saying: "From beginningless time, from life to life, all sentient beings have had their disturbing illusions that have been manifested in their natural development each under the conditioning power of his own individual Karma, such as the seed-pod of the okra which when opening always drops three seeds in each group.

"The reason why all devoted disciples do not at once attain to supreme enlightenment is they do not realize the Two Primary Principles and because of it some attain only to limited saintship, or to partial understanding of the novice, and some become confused in mind and fall into wrong practices. It is as if they were trying to cook fine delicacies by boiling stones or sand which of course they could never do if they tried for countless kalpas of time.

"These two Fundamental Principles are:

"One, the primary cause of the succession of deaths and rebirths from beginningless time. From the working out of this Principle there has resulted the various differentiation of minds of all sentient beings, and all the time they have been taking these limited and perturbed and contaminated minds to be their true and natural Essence of Mind.

"Two, the primary cause of the pure unity of Enlightenment

and Nirvana that has existed from beginningless time. By the indrawing of this Principle within the brightness of your own nature, its unifying spirit can be discovered and developed and realized under all varieties of conditions. The reason why this unifying spirit is so quickly lost amongst the conditions is because you so quickly forget the brightness and purity of your own essential nature, and amid the activities of the day, you cease to realize its existence. That is why, Ananda, you and all sentient beings have fallen through ignorance into misfortune and into different realms of existence."

The Tathagata raised one of his arms with hand and fingers clenched, saying: "Ananda, while you are looking at my fist closely, what is it that reveals the existence of your Essential Mind?"

Ananda replied: "This thinking and reasoning being which enables me to perceive your shining fist, is what is meant as 'my mind.'"

The Buddha rebuked Ananda sharply and said: "Surely that is nonsense, to assert that your being is your mind."

Ananda stood up with hands pressed together and said with astonishment: "Why, my Lord, if my being is not my mind, what else can be my mind? Myself is my mind! If I should give up my perceptions and consciousness, there would be nothing left that could be regarded as myself or my mind."

Thereupon the Blessed One laid his hand affectionately upon the head of Ananda: "Now that I have removed my fist, and its sight has vanished from your thinkings and reasonings, does your mind vanish, also, and become like hair on a tortoise, or a horn on a rabbit?

"Since your mind goes on discriminating the memory of those perceptions and consciousness of my fist, it has not vanished.

"Ananda and all my disciples! With reference to Ananda saying that his mind is himself, I have always taught you that all phenomena is simply a manifestation of mind essence. So it is with what you call, self, it is simply a manifestation of mind essence.

"If we examine the origin of anything in all the universe, we find that it is but a manifestation of some primal essence. Even the tiny leaves of herbs, knots of thread, everything, if we examine these carefully we find that there is some essence in its originality.

"The essence of ripples on the sea, is the sea. Just so, the essence of thoughts in the mind, is the mind.

"Self and objects and developments of self, are not permanent, like all objects and thoughts, which are as ripples; as they vanish, should I ask again does your mind essence vanish, also, and become like hair on a tortoise, or a horn on a rabbit?

"If the mind essence vanished there would be nothing and no sentient beings to discuss it.

"The mind essence does not vanish because it transcends and is beyond phenomena and is free from all discriminating thoughts of self and not-self.

"As soon as the mind discriminates, all causes and effects from the great universes on down to the fine dust only seen in the sunlight, come into apparent existence, like ripples forming on the surface of the sea.

"This we know about ripples on the surface of the sea, and that is to say, about this apparently existing world which we see like ripples on the surface of the sea of Universal Mind Essence: we know that the ripples bear the three marks of existence. These three marks of existence that the ripples bear, are, one, Transiency, their being short-lived; two, Infelicity, their being troubled, non-peaceful, and ever changing; and three, Unreality, their having no substantial existence in themselves as ripples, being mere manifestations of form in water due to wind. In the same way this phenomenal world is mere manifestation of Mind Essence due to Ignorance.

"Therefore, Ananda, what revealed the existence of your Essential Mind when you looked at my fist, was neither yes or no the appearance of my fist as discriminated by your discriminating mind, for both of these are just ripples on the surface;

naturally, it is your Essential Mind that is the basis, as the sea for the waves, in this revelation of sight.

"As long as you grasp this brain-mind of discriminating consciousness that is dependent upon the different sense organs as being the same as Essential Mind, as long as you grasp at this deceiving conception of discriminative thinking that is based on unrealities, as long as you go on mistaking the delusion as being the reality, you will not be free from the intoxicants arising from worldly contaminations and attachments and will ever be in bondage to the wheel of grief in this transmigratory, evil, Sangsara world, which is as but a smirch in the shining reality."

Ananda was in tears and sorrowful and apologized for his great learning and his great vexation too, which he called the two great hindrances.

Again the Buddha made a fist and held it up in the bright sunshine: "By what means does the brightness of the sight of this fist manifest itself?"

Ananda: "Because of the brightness I see it with my eyes and my mind conceives its brightness."

Buddha: "Does your perception of sight depend on brightness?"

Ananda: "Without brightness I wouldn't see anything."

Buddha: "In his blindness a blind man sees darkness and nothing else. There is no loss of his conception of sight but his conception is of darkness. He simply sees as any seeing man who is shut up in a dark room. Close your eyes, Ananda, what do you perceive but darkness?"

Ananda admitted that he perceived the darkness.

Buddha: "If the blind man were suddenly to recover his sight, it would be as though a lamp had been brought into a dark room and we would say that the man again sees objects by means of the lamp. But the perception of sight, perception itself, does not depend on either of these two arbitrary conceptions of brightness or darkness, nor on the lamp, nor on the eyes, because the perception of sight, perception itself, originates in your Essential Original Perfect Mind. Essential Mind transcends and abides throughout phenomena of causes and conditions such as brightness, darkness, eyes, and lamps, and is free from them and responds freely to them as their occasion arises, just like the sea transcends and abides throughout its ripples yet responds freely to them as their occasion of rippling arises.

"In a true sense, therefore, it is neither conception of brightness in your mind, nor your eyes, that perceived my fist."

Ananda sat dazed hoping for a clearer interpretation of this instruction in the kind and gentle tones of the Master and he waited with a pure and expectant heart.

The Blessed One, in great kindness, let his hand rest kindly on the head of Ananda and said to him: "The reason why all sentient beings fail to attain enlightenment until they become Buddhas, is because they have been led astray by false conceptions regarding phenomena and objects, which defiled their minds. Deeply absorbed in their dream, they cannot wake up to the reality of the perfect bright emptiness of their Essential Mind which is everywhere. They do not know that everything is seen of the mind itself.

"They concentrate on the dream instead of on the Mind that makes it.

"Essential Mind is like open space, permanent and motionless; the dream of existence is like particles of dust shifting and appearing and disappearing in open space.

"Essential Mind is like the inn; but the dream of existence is like the impermanent traveler who can only stay overnight and has to move on, ever-changing.

The Buddha, raising his hand, opened his fingers and then closed them: "Ananda, what is in motion and what is still?"

Ananda saw that it was the Blessed One's hand opening and closing, not his "seeing" that moved. "My Lord, it was the fingers that were in motion, not the perception of my eyes."

"Ananda," said the Buddha, "can you not see the difference in nature in that which moves and changes, and that which is motionless and unchanging? It is body which moves and changes, not Mind.

"Why do you so persistently look upon motion as appertaining to body and mind both? Why do you permit your thoughts to rise and fall, letting the body rule the mind, instead of Mind ruling the body?

"Why do you let your senses deceive you as to the true unchanging nature of Mind and then to do things in a reversed order in the direction of the Principle of Ignorance which leads to motion and confusion and suffering?

"As one forgets the true nature of Mind, so he mistakes the ripple-like objects on its illimitable bosom as being his whole mind, he mistakes the reflections of objects as being his own mind, thus binding him to the endless restless movements and impermanent changes and suffering of the recurrent cycles of deaths and rebirths that are of his own causing.

"You should regard all that changes as 'dust-particles' and that which is unchanging as being your own true Nature of Mind."

Then Ananda and all the assembly realized that from beginningless time, they had forgotten and ignored their own true nature amongst the illusive reflections of the world and the world was mind-only. They felt like a little baby that had found its mother's breast, and became calm and peaceful in spirit. They besought the Lord Tathagata to teach them how to make right distinctions between body and mind, between the real and the unreal, between that which is true and that which is false, between the manifested natures of deaths and rebirths on the one hand, and the intrinsic nature of that which is un-born and never dies on the other hand; the one appearing and disappearing, the other forever abiding within the essence of their own mind.

King Prasenajit rose and asked the Buddha for some instruction that would enable him to realize the nature of no-dying and no-rebirth, so that he could begin to understand the state that ultimately freed one from the wheel of deaths and rebirths. The Buddha asked him to describe his present appearance as compared with his appearance in boyhood. The King cried: "How can I compare my present with my youth?" and described the gradual process of decay and change year by year, month by month, "yes, day by day," that would soon end in his complete destruction. Then the Buddha asked him how old he was when he first saw the River Ganges, age three; and the second time, age thirteen; and how old he was now, age sixty-two; and if his perception of the Ganges had changed. The King replied: "The sight of my eyes is not as good, but my perception of the sight is just the same as ever."

The Buddha addressed him: "Your Majesty! You have been saddened by the changes in your personal appearance since your youth—your greying hair and wrinkled face, your failing blood-supply—but you say that your perception of sight compared with it when you were a youth, shows no change. Tell me, Your Majesty, is there any youth and old age in the perception of sight?"

"Not at all, your Lordship."

The Buddha continued: "Your Majesty! Though your face has become wrinkled, in the perception of your eyes, there are no signs of age, no wrinkles. Then, wrinkles are the symbol of change, and the un-wrinkled is the symbol of the un-changing. That which is changing must suffer destruction, but the un-changing is free from deaths and rebirths."

Everyone in the assembly was greatly cheered to hear this ancient news from the Tathagata and to begin to realize its mysterious truth.

Then Ananda wanted to know why it was, since the perception of the Mind is free from deaths and rebirths, nevertheless people forget their true nature of Mind and act in a state of "reversed confusion" in the direction of the Principle of Ignorance.

The Buddha held out his arm with fingers pointing downward in some mystic <u>mudra</u>. "Ananda, if this position is called 'reversed,' what would you call upright?"

"Lord, putting the fingers up would be called 'upright.'"

The Buddha suddenly turned his hand and said to Ananda: "If this interpretation of positions, reversed or upright, is simply made by turning the hand so that the fingers are pointing either up or down without any change in the location of the hand, that is, as viewed by beings in this world, then you should know that the universal essence of Mind which is everywhere forever everything, which is the Womb of Tathagata, which is the pure Dharmakaya (Body of the Established Law), may be interpreted differently by viewing it from different view points of attainment, as being either Nirvana unborn beyond existence, the Tathagata's 'True Enlightenment' (bright, perfect, empty, immortal), or as Sangsara, conditional existence, the world we have, mortal, impure, dark, suffering, the apparitions of ignorance in one's own discriminating brain-mind, the 'reversed position.'"

Ananda and the whole assembly were confused and stared up at him with open mouths. What did he mean by a reversed position of mind? Yet the reason they were now seeing him with their eyes instead of seeing merely nothing in the pure true void, was verily because of this reversed position of their minds.

In great compassion of heart, the Buddha pitied Ananda and the great assembly. He spoke to them reassuringly: "My good faithful disciples! Have I not been constantly teaching you that all of the causes and conditions that characterize changing phenomena and the modes of the mind, and of the different attributes of the mind, and the independently developed conditions of the mind, are all simply manifestations of the mind; and all of your body and mind are but manifestations of the wonderful, enlightening, and true nature of the all-embracing and mysterious Essence of Mind.

"Everything is taking place in your mind, like a dream.

"As soon as you wake up and stop dreaming, your mind returns to its original emptiness and purity.

"In truth, your mind has already returned to its original emptiness and purity, and this world is but a limping shadow.

"Why do you still so easily forget this natural, wonderful, and enlightened Mind of perfect Purity—this mysterious Mind of radiant Brightness?

"And why are you still bewildered in your realizing consciousness?"

Whereupon the Buddha in a few brief words described the Genesis of the World: "Open space is nothing but invisible dimness; the invisible dimness of space is mingled with darkness to look like forms; sensations of form are turned into illusive and arbitrary conceptions of phenomena; and from these false inventive conceptions of phenomena, is developed the consciousness of body.

"So, within the mind, narrowing finally to the brain mind of the self, these jumblings of causes and conditions, segregating into groups and coming into contact with the projected objects of the world, there is awakened desire or fear which divides the mind of original undisturbability and causes it to excite to either passion or panic, to either indulgence or anger. All of you have been accepting this confusing self-conscious conception as being your own nature of mind.

"As soon as you accepted it as your true mind, is it any wonder that you became bewildered and supposed it to be localized in your physical body and that all the external things, mountains, rivers, the great open spaces, and the whole world, were outside the body.

"Is it any wonder that you failed to realize that everything you have so falsely conceived has its only existence within your own wonderful, enlightening Mind of True Essence.

In likeness you have abandoned all the great, pure, calm oceans of water, and clung to one ripple which you not only accept but which you regard as the whole body of water in all the hundreds of thousands of seas. In such bewilderment you reveal yourselves as fools among fools. Though I move my finger up or down, there is no change in the hand itself. Though you forget the true nature of mind or not, there is no change in the true nature of mind. But the world makes a distinction, and says that now the hand is upright, now it is reversed, that now the true nature of mind is Nirvana-purity, now it is Sangsara-defilement. Since Essence is beyond conception of any kind, those who do this are greatly to be pitied."

Ananda, realizing that his Essential Mind was the permanent ground for his changing discriminating brain-mind, wanted to know if the mind with which he was individuating and discriminating his Lord's teaching about Essential Mind was the same as his Essential Mind.

The Buddha replied: "Ananda, when in my teaching I point my finger at the moon, you take my finger to be the moon. If you take that which discriminated my teaching as your mind, then when it lays aside its conceptions of the discriminated teaching, the mind should still retain its own discriminating nature, which it does not.

"It is like a traveller seeking an inn where he may rest for a short time but not permanently. But the inn-keeper lives there permanently, he does not go away. It is the same with this difficulty. If the discriminating brain-mind is your True Mind, it should never change and go away. How can it be your True Mind when, as soon as the sound of my voice ceases, it has no discriminating nature?

"Both your brain-mind, which is like a ripple, and its Essence, which is like the sea, have one individual and original nature which is the one and true reality."

Ananda said: "Noble Lord, if both my discriminating brain-mind and its Essence have one originality, why does the Essential Mind which is like the sea, which has just been proclaimed by the Lord Buddha as being one with my discriminating brain-mind, why does it not return to its original state?" But as soon as he asked this Ananda realized that he was talking about an originality that has no need of returning.

And now the Buddha proceeded to elaborate the teaching that would free the assembled devotees from bondage to false perception.

"There is no brightness in actuality, except as it is the perception of brightness:- for what's bright to the door?

"Brightness is not caused by the sun, it's simply that the sun makes it possible for there to be perception of brightness in open space. Where do you return the perception of brightness to? Not to the sun. To the perceiving mind.

"Because if you returned the faculty of perceiving to the sun, and said that it originated in the sun, then when the sun is gone down and there is no brightness, then there would be no perception of darkness. Perception is our Essential Mind; the sun's brightness or the dim moon's darkness are the conditional ripples on its surface.

"What does your ear know of brightness or darkness? What does your eye know of silence or sound? So you should know, the phenomena that the sense-organs perceive does not originate in the reality of Essential Mind but in the senses themselves.

"For instance, Ananda, the brightness of the sun that your

eyes perceive does not originate in the reality of Essential Mind, which is neither in brightness or darkness, but exists exclusively for your eyes and in your eyes themselves.

"And you may know, Ananda, the fire burning for centuries up there, which we call the sun, that your eyes, body, and brain-mind perceive, does not originate in the reality of Essential Mind which is the Holy Void and beyond all conditons of fire and absence of fire, but exists exclusively for the eyes, body, and brain-mind, and in the eyes, body, and brain-mind themselves.

"Ananda, if you had no body, for you there could be no earth and you could pass through it. That is your sun.

"Ananda, in reality, it's just as foolish to say, that there is no body and no earth, as to say that there is a body and an earth: for all is empty and a vision throughout. That is your sun."

These mysterious words frightened the disciples who wanted a simple explanation, whereupon the Buddha, always obeying the universal intrinsic sincerity in the essence-heart of this ignorant world, complied with their earnest wishes.

"My good and faithful disciples, in answer to Ananda's request as to how he can fully realize that the nature of his mind's perceiving, which is constant and deeply unruffled by seeming phenomena, is his true and essential nature, I shall ask him to go to the extreme limit of sight with me, that is, I will abandon my Tathagata sight which freely reaches everywhere through all the Buddha-lands of Purity greater in number than the fine particles of dust, and go with Ananda to the palaces of the sun and moon—do you see anything there that belongs to our true and essential nature? Coming nearer to the Seven Golden Mountains that surround Mt. Sumeru, look carefully, what do you see? We see all sorts of brightness and glory, but nothing that belongs to our true and essential nature. Moving nearer, we come to the massing clouds, the flying birds, the hurrying winds, the rising of dust, the mountains, the familiar woods, trees, rivers, herbs, vegetables, animals, none of which belongs to our true and essential nature.

"Ananda, regarding all those things, far or near, as perceived by the pure Essence of your perceiving eyes, they have different characteristics, but the perception of our eyes is always the same. Does this not mean, that this wonderful essence of the perception of sight neither fixed nor changeable is the true nature of our minds?"

Thereupon Ananda wanted to know if since the essence of the perception of sight naturally permeates the whole universe, why was it that now as he and the Buddha sat in the Hall their perception of sight was partitioned off by walls and houses?

"Ananda," replied the Buddha, "it is not an attribute of the essence of our perception of sight that walls are up and so the eyes can't see through their impenetrability, or that walls are down and the eyes can see across open space, or that it is bright and so the eyes can see brightness, or that it is dark and so eyes can see darkness. This changeableness is not an attribute of our true perception of sight which is our wonderful, enlightening Essential Mind which, like space, is neither changeable nor fixed.

"Ananda, the appearance of the wall does not hide the true emptiness, the true emptiness does not annihilate the appearance of the wall."

Then the Buddha continued, saying: "Suppose, Ananda, that you and I are looking out over the gardens, even to the sun and moon, and seeing all the multitudinous objects, and no such 'thing' as the perception of sight can be pointed out to us. But, Ananda, among all these multitudinous phenomena, can you show me anything which does not belong to the perception of sight?"

Ananda replied: "Noble Lord! True, I am convinced now that all objects whatsoever, be they little or big, wherever there are manifestations and appearances, all belong to the perception of sight."

The Buddha expressed agreement, saying: "So it is, Ananda, so it is."

Then all the junior disciples, except the older ones among them who had finished the practice of meditation, having listened to the discussion and not understanding the significance of the conclusion, became confused and frightened and lost control of themselves.

The Tathagata consoled them: "My good, pious disciples! All that the supreme Teacher of the Dharma has taught are true and sincere words, they are neither extravagant nor fancies and chimerical. They are not to be compared with the puzzling paradoxes propounded like riddles by the famous heretic teacher. Do not be disturbed by what has been taught, but ponder upon it seriously and never give yourself up either to sadness or delight."

Then Manjusri rose up and wanted for the sake of the others to have the ambiguity cleared up, as to whether the things that we see exist for, and belong to, the perception of sight, saying, "For these Brothers the explanation needs to be very plain."

The Buddha replied: "Manjusri and all my good Disciples: Why should there be any ambiguity as to belonging or not belonging, between the perception of sight which is the ocean, and the seeing of things which is the ripples on that same ocean?

"The Tathagatas in the ten quarters of the universe, whether they teach with words or without, together with all the Great Wise Beings, as they are intrinsically abiding in Ecstasy, regard all of the seeings of things, their causes and conditions, and all of the conceptions about them, as being visionary flowers in the air, having no true nature of existence within themselves because they partake of the quick infelicitous imaginary state of cause-arisen ripples.

"The wonderful, enlightening perception of sight, the see-ing of objects as well as objects themselves, they all intrinsically belong to the pure, perfect Essential Mind.

"Therefore, when one is looking upon these manifestations, which are visionary flowers arising from the senses in contact with objects, he must remember that they are all illusion and then there will be no ambiguity."

Then Ananda, professing his faith in the Buddha's teaching that pure perception of sight itself was his original Essential Mind and all the variegated sights in themselves belonged to it only in essence because they had no self-nature but were like ripples coming and going as ignorance dictated, now wanted to know exactly how all this worked so that he could apprehend with his own mind what his heart already believed with respect to the reliability of the Buddha's teaching.

Thereupon the Buddha explained how the false perception of the eyes worked. "Ananda, it is the eyes, not the intrinsic perception of Mind, that is subject to false mistakes. A man with sick eyes sees lamp halo but it is not his undisturbable Essential Mind that developed the halo, it is his brain-mind discriminat-ing according to the eyes that are sick. In the same way, healthy eyes see imaginary balls and traveling blossoms in empty space.

So you will know, it is because eyes are naturally invested with false perception of sight that everything that you see with your eyes is a false ripple. This has been so with eyesight since beginningless time; the very fact that you have eyesight is part of your Karma, your inheritance from ignorant deeds done elsewhere.

"But Ananda do not be disturbed. Since it is just a matter of time that you will shed this eyesight, then you have already shed this eyesight.

"Ananda, not only the sense organ known as your eyes, but the other five sense organs of ears, nose, tongue, body, and brain, are by nature false and fantastic and continue to fool you as you live and breathe.

"Let me show you how all six organs work to delude you and make you forget the bright, perfect, mysterious, divine Emptiness of your true and Essential Mind.

"When you look at empty space in the day sky, you immediately begin to see imaginary little balls and traveling blossoms; other strange sights such as particles of the sun's burning energy can be seen coming on and off like little lights, but these cosmic particles seem to belong to the sun's energy; but where do the imaginary blossoms have their source? Ananda, they are false and fantastic appearances pure and simple. And why? Because if these imaginary blossoms belonged to the eyesight naturally they would have the power of seeing, they would be like your eyesight and being out there in plain view of your eyes you could see yourself with them. Or if, then, they belonged to empty space, they would be coming from and going somewhere else in empty space and hiding in empty space and so you could no longer say that it was empty space. Be sure, it is empty space, and by looking, perception was roused from dreamless sleep in the deeps of Essential Mind, and the seeing of sights was made manifest. Ananda, the imaginary blossoms are indications of the sick condition of morbid mist which we call 'good eyesight' and which has been instrumental in making sentient beings pitiful dupes of false sights since beginningless time.

"It is the same with your perception of feeling, it is the false perception of the body."

"How so, my Lord?"

"Ananda, it is the body, not the intrinsic perception of Mind that is subject to false mistakes. A man with sick body feels pain, but it is not his undisturbable Essential Mind that developed the pain, it is his brain-mind discriminating according to the body that is sick. In the same way, healthy bodies feel touch, which is imaginary, in empty space. So you will know, it is because body is naturally invested with false perception of touch that everything that you feel with your body is a false ripple. This has been so with body since beginningless time; the very fact that you have a body is part of your Karma, your inheritance from ignorant deeds done elsewhere.

"But Ananda do not be disturbed. Since it is just a matter of time that you'll shed this body, then you have already shed this body.

"When you rub your hands together, and feel sensations of smoothness and warmth, or roughness and coldness, where does this perception of feeling have its source? Ananda, it is a completely false and fantastic feeling pure and simple. And why? Because if this feeling of touch belonged to the hands themselves naturally they would manifest that sensation of touch all the time and would not have to wait for a rubbing-together. Or if, then, the feeling of touch belonged not to the body but to that which is not the body, empty space, it would be felt all over the body all the time and not just in the rubbing hands.

"Be sure, it is empty space, and by touching, perception was roused from dreamless sleep in the deeps of Essential Mind, and the feeling of touch was made manifest. Ananda, the feeling of touch is an indication of the sick condition of morbid mist which we call 'healthy body' and which has been instrumental in making sentient beings pitiful dupes of false feelings since beginningless time.

"It is the same with your perception of hearing; it is the false perception of the ears."

"How so, my Lord?"

"Ananda, it is the ears, not the intrinsic perception of Mind, that is subject to false mistakes. A man with sick ears hears a roaring in his head, but it is not his undisturbable Essential Mind that developed the roaring, it is his brain-mind discriminating according to the ears that are sick. In the same way, healthy ears hear sound, which is imaginary, in empty space. So you will know, it is because ears are naturally invested with false perception of sound that everything that you hear with your ears is a false ripple. This has been so with ears since beginningless time; the very fact that you have ears is part of your Karma, your inheritance from ignorant deeds done elsewhere.

"But Ananda do not be disturbed. Since it is just a matter of time that you will shed these ears, then you have already shed these ears.

"When you hear me strike my gong, the so-called vibrations beat against your ear-drum and you perceive the sound of the gong, but where does this so-called sound have its source? Ananda, it is a completely false and fantastic sound pure and simple. And why? Because if this sound had its source in your ears naturally it would not be in the gong, and your ears would be aware of sound all the time and would not have to wait for a banging of gongs. Or if then, the sound belonged to the gong and depended on the gong and had its source in the gong, and it was the motion of the sound-waves from the gong, that was developing the sound, how then would your ears know it any more than the stick that strikes the gong? If the sound came from neither the ears nor the gong it would be like the imaginary blossoms in the sky, a fantasy in empty space, ripples that sentient beings discriminate and name as sound. The wise cease to regard appearances and names as realities. When appearances and names are put away and all discrimination ceases, that which remains is the true and essential nature of things and, as nothing can be predicated as to the nature of essence, it is called the 'Suchness' of Reality. This universal, undifferentiated, inscrutable 'Suchness' is the only Reality but it is variously characterized as Truth, Mind-essence, Transcendental Intelligence, Noble Wisdom and so forth. This law of the imagelessness and soundlessness of the Essence-nature of Ultimate Reality is the Law which has been proclaimed by all the Buddhas. As soon as the whimsical banging and clapping and noisy motions of the world cease, then the imagination of sound ceases, but the essence of the Hearing-nature remains as potential and pure as empty space. Be sure, it is empty space, and by my striking the gong, perception was roused from dreamless sleep in the deeps of Essential Mind and the hearing of sound was made manifest.

"As to sounds, which are ripples, you may insist that ripples are real, but because they are ripples they will soon become no-ripples, and therefore they are already not ripples in Ultimate Reality.

"Ananda, the hearing of sound is an indication of the sick conditon of morbid mist which we call 'good ears' and which has been instrumental in making sentient beings pitiful dupes of false sounds since beginningless time.

"It is the same with your perception of smelling, it is the false perception of the nose."

"How so, my Lord?"

"Ananda, it is the nose, not the intrinsic perception of Mind that is subject to false mistakes. A man with a sick nose smells some unpleasant metallic odor, but it is not his undisturbable Essential Mind that developed the odor, it is his brain-mind discriminating according to the nose that is sick. In the same way, a healthy nose smells odor, which is imaginary, in empty space. So you will know, it is because the nose is naturally invested with false perception of odor that everything that you smell with your nose is a false ripple. This has been so with the nose since beginningless time; the very fact that you have a nose is part of your Karma, your inheritance from ignorant deeds done elsewhere.

"But Ananda do not be disturbed. Since it's just a matter of time that you will shed this nose, then you've already shed this nose.

"Blossoms of flowers are soft explosions of their short-lived selves. When these flowers are placed before you, the extremely passible particles of the blossom pass through space and come against the impassible receiver of your nose and you become aware of a perception of fragrance, but where does this phenomena of fragrance have its source? Ananda, it is a completely false and fantastic odor pure and simple. And why? Because if this odor had its source in the nose, why does the nose have to wait till the flowers are brought before it, for it to become aware of the fragrance of flowers? If this odor had its source in the nose, the nose would be smelling that odor all the time and the phenomena of the odor would not be subject to accidents and conditions like placing the flowers before you. So the odor must have its source in the flowers, but why is it that the phenomena of this odor has to have a nose and the conditions of a nose to pick it up and discriminate it as odor? Or why doesn't the odor manifest itself to the eyes, or the ears? For if the flowers and odor had self-nature, all space would be one fragrance. So if, then, the odor of the flowers had its source not in your nose but in the empty space between your nose and the flowers, you would have to say that the odor is coming from somewhere and going somewhere else, since it appears and disappears, and hiding in empty space, and you could no longer call it empty space. Be sure it is empty space, and by smelling the flowers, universal perception was roused from dreamless sleep in the deeps of Essential Mind, and the smelling of odor appeared according to the individual condition of nose.

"Ananda, this smelling of odor is an indication of the sick condition of morbid mist which we call 'good nose' and which has been instrumental in making sentient beings pitiful dupes of false odors since beginningless time, causing them to turn around and do things in a reversed order.

"And the same with your perception of tasting, it is the false perception of the tongue."

"How so, my Lord?"

"Ananda, what does the curry sauce taste to the wooden bowl? Ananda, it is the tongue, not the intrinsic perception of Mind that is subject to false mistakes. A man with a sick tongue tastes some unpleasant cottony taste, but it is not his undisturbable Essential Mind that developed the taste, it is his brain-mind discriminating according to the tongue that is sick. In the same way, a healthy tongue tastes flavor, which is imaginary, in empty space. So you will know, it is because the tongue is naturally invested with false perception of flavor that everything that you taste with your tongue is a false ripple. This has been so with the tongue since beginningless time; the very fact that you have a tongue is part of your Karma, your inheritance from ignorant deeds done elsewhere.

"But Ananda do not be disturbed. Since it is just a matter of time that you'll shed this tongue, then you have already shed this tongue.

"When the curry sauce comes into contact with your palate, and whether it is my palate or yours we both taste the spiciness, the highly changeable elements and their condiments are received by the taste-ducts of the tongue and the perception of flavor emerges and according to our habit energies we say it tastes 'good' or it tastes 'bad,' but where does this so-called flavor have its source? Ananda, it is a completely false and fantastic flavor pure and simple. And why? Because if this flavor had its source in the tongue, naturally it would not need the incident of the sauce to taste the flavor of the sauce, but we see that this takes place only when the sauce is put in the mouth. Or if, then, the flavor had its source in the sauce, how then would the tongue know it any more than the wooden bowl? Ananda, the flavor is a fantasy in empty space, and by tasting of the sauce, universal perception was roused from dreamless sleep in Essential Mind, and the tasting of flavor made its appearance according to the individual tongue.

"Ananda, the tasting of flavor is an indication of the sick condition of morbid mist which we call 'good tongue' and which has been instrumental in making sentient beings pitiful dupes of false flavors since beginningless time, causing them grief.

"And the same with your perception of thinking, it is the false perception of the brain."

"How so, my Lord?"

"Ananda, it is the brain, not the intrinsic perception of Mind, that is subject to false mistakes. A man with a sick brain thinks that his head has become a goblin but it is not his undisturbable crystal clear Essential Mind that developed this thought, it is his brain-mind discriminating according to the brain that is sick. In the same way, healthy brains think thoughts, which are imaginary, in empty space. So you will know, it is because the brain is naturally invested with the false perception of discriminative thinking that everything that you conceive of with your brain is a false ripple. Ananda, the intuitive self-realization of Noble Wisdom that comes with Transcendental Intelligence that reveals the True and Essential Mind, which has ever been an inconceivable activity of the Buddha-nature of purity permeating everywhere and always, in other words, that which happens when a sentient being sees the Light which was previously obscured by his brain as moon by cloud, is not an individualized discriminative thought appearing in the brain of that bubble known as Ananda's self. False and busy thinking that leads one to the gloom of Ignorance and Karma, the very perception of the brain, has been so since beginningless time; the very fact that you have a brain and that it developed since your so-called birth, is part of your Karma, your inheritance from conditioned, impure deeds of this world done elsewhere in ignorance.

"But Ananda do not be disturbed. Since it's just a matter of time that you will shed this brain, then you have already shed this brain.

"It is because of the opposing, dual, and therefore false and conditional conceptions of appearance and disappearance that the brain makes out thoughts. Just like healthy eyes that develop fantastic blossoms in the sky which nevertheless do not belong to the eyes nor to the sky and are perfectly imaginary, the brain develops thoughts that come and go which nevertheless do not belong to the brain nor to anything and are perfectly imaginary. Where do these millions of thoughts that pass in a continual parade in the Seven Kinds of Swiftness across the dark amphitheater of your brain have their source? Ananda, each one of these billions of bubbles are of one Essence, Essence of Mind, and is a completely false and fantastic thought pure and simple. And why? Because if a passing thought had its source in the brain, and the thought belonged to your brain, why should it vanish and make way for millions of others like it, each one an additional and transitory and soon-to-be-unrippled ripple, as for instance, a thought about taking a voyage, which is followed immediately by a thought of what to have for dinner. Surely these are real dreams, but Ananda they are dreams! Or if, a thought had its source anywhere else outside the brain, then, supposing there was no brain, it would be clear that the thought could not exist independently of the brain, which means the same thing as saying that the thought is completely false and fantastic.

"Be sure, it is all a spectral tissue in empty space, and by discriminating the appearance and disappearance of thoughts in your brain, universal perception was roused from dreamless sleep in the deeps of Essential Mind, in the imageless bliss of it, responded with perfect accommodation, and the thinking of thoughts appeared according to the troublous individual conditions of brain.

"Ananda, the thinking of thoughts is an indication of the sick condition of morbid mist which we call 'good mind,' and which has been instrumental in making sentient beings pitiful dupes of false thoughts since beginningless time, causing them to act in the direction of deaths and rebirths and so perpetuating their circumambient enslavement to the awful wheel of sorrowful existence.

"Those who have attained enlightenment, and have ceased to notice that which does not necessarily exist, that is, existence itself, which they see clearly as a bubble that for all intents and purposes has already burst, are as if awakening from sleep, and their past life seems only a dream."

Though Ananda in his heart of hearts was made implicitly and truthfully aware of the import of this teaching that the six senses are false and fantastic, still in his thinking-mind he had not yet resolved speculative dilemmas concerning the apparent solidity and substantialness of such elements as Earth, Water, Fire and Wind and their continual transformations, which according to his Lord's previous teaching were perfectly imaginary manifestations of Illimitable Essential Mind and nothing else.

So he inquired respectfully on the subject, and by his perfect silence and attention, showed himself ready for the teaching from the Blessed One.

The Buddha said: "Ananda, it is just as you have said, all the varieties and changes in this world with which the subjective six senses appear to assume objective contact, are manifested by means of the combining and the conforming of the Four Great Elements (earth, water, fire, air); there are three other Great Elements, namely, Space, Perception, and Consciousness, making, in all, Seven Great Elements. Let us begin with the earth-element.

"Why is the earth a bubble? Ananda, does it fit the case to question whether the center of a bubble is empty or not empty? Because the earth is made up of infinitesimal particles of dust that can be analyzed down to the atom and the atom of that, infinitely, each atom in likeness to our universe, to the universe and the universe of that, so that wise men know there are universes in their little eye lash more numerous than all the sands in whole unnumerable Ganges-sands of Ganges Rivers. Ananda, what is happening in these vast and spectral spaces, anyway?

"Look carefully! Stare through the sight of things and you will only see the Great Heart of Compassion of all the Buddhas of Old beyond belief. This is <u>Yathabhutam</u>, the seeing of things truly.

"Consider the nature of the earth element. In a crude and coarse form it covers the globe, but in a highly refined form it is the infinitesimal dust of space, and even everything that the eyes can see can be reduced into its primal elements, so that all that is seen as sight is earth. You should know, Ananda, that if this earth, this infinitesimal dust of space, should truly be reduced to the purity and emptiness of space, it would be out of this inconceivable purity that the phenomena of sight is manifested also.

"Ananda, the intrinsic nature of earth is the real emptiness of space, the true vacuum; while the intrinsic nature of space is the real earth, the true essence.

"In the Tathagata's Womb of the un-bornness of the un-born essence of all things which is the Ultimate and Supreme Reality, space and sights are of perennial freshness and purity, permeating everywhere throughout the phenomenal universes, and are being forever manifested spontaneously and perfectly in accordance with the amount of Karma-need accumulated under the conscious activity of sentient beings who are but pitiful forms of ignorance in what is like a vision and a dream a long time already finished. However, people of the world, spectral giants inside mind, being ignorant of the principle that governs their own existence, become bewildered in the entanglements of causes and conditions and naturalism, they think the earth carries signs of an inherent self-nature of its own and call it 'natural' and 'Mother Nature' with all the mental trees independent of their own bodies, they think that it exists due to causes such as creation by some self-created and self-remembering Creator Self who made them after his own image and that their existence comes under the conditions of 'time,' atoms, seasons, celestial interventions, personal destiny, all of which are wholly the discriminations of their mental consciousness and are merely figurative words having no meaning in reality.

"Ananda, where does this infinitesimal dust come from, this earth, and how does it sojourn here? It's as if someone had suddenly given you a free store and said 'How much earth do you want? How much sight do you want?' Yet you did not truly want. Everywhere is the place where earth originates. Earth obeys and earth is everywhere. That is, earth is proof of the fact that molecular properties and combinations always assist in the appearance of earth. Earth responds to combinations that we may understand by analysis of molecular properties but these combinations are not its place of origination or its cause. What was the original condition before it was attracted and combined and became earth? Essential Mind is the essence and the source of the phenomena of earth."

Ananda said to the Buddha: "Pray tell us about the Water element, my Noble Lord."

The Blessed One replied: "Why is water a dream, Ananda? Does it fit the case to question whether a dream is real or unreal?

"Ananda, let us consider the nature of the Water element. By nature water is impermanent, whether in the current of rivers or in the waves of the sea. When the sun comes up at dawn, and heats the mist, the mist drops water-beads into the cup. What do you think about it, Ananda? Does this water come from the mist, or does it come out of space, or does it really come from the sun? If it came from the sun, then every time the sun shines there would be water everywhere, but as it is we see there has to be mist as well. If it came from the mist, then why did it have to wait till sunrise to distill into water? But if you had such mist and no water come from it, it would be proof that water does not come from the sun. If the water comes from the empty space between the sun and the mist, then, as space is boundless and if water was equally boundless, then all sentient beings on earth or in sky would be in danger of drowning. If you were to say that water came from all three combined, you would be saying that water had its source in the sun, in the mist and in the vast space between them, which makes three sources. From where does the water come from? Surely it cannot come from nowhere. And then, again, consider that wherever mist may be standing in the sunrise in some one place there water appears, supposing there is mist all over the world and water is appearing everywhere, what would that signify?

"Ananda! Why is it that you still remain in ignorance that the intrinsic nature of water is the real emptiness, while the intrinsic nature of space is the real water-essence.

"In the reality of the Shining Emptiness that is the Essence of Mind, both water and space abide in freshness and purity and in essence obtain everywhere throughout the universes and are being manifested freely, and perfectly corresponding to the accumulation and inheritance of Karma by the conscious activity of sentient beings.

"However, people of this world, being ignorant of this, and by regarding water as being made to appear by means of causes and conditions exclusively or spontaneously by its own self-nature, have become bewildered. Whereas, all of these false presuppositions and prejudices are simply the discriminations made by their own mental consciousness, and are merely figurative words having no basis in reality.

"Where does water come from, and how does it sojourn here? Everywhere is the place where water originates; that is, water responds to combinations such as distillation of mist at sunrise, but this combination is not the place of origination of water. Essential Mind is the essence and the source of the phenomena of water."

Ananda said to the Blessed One: "Pray tell us, my Noble Lord, about the fire-element."

The Blessed One replied: "Why is fire an idea, Ananda? Does it fit the case to question whether a thought has appeared or disappeared?

"Ananda, let us consider the element of fire. Fire has not its own individual nature, but is dependent on other considerations. If you were to look towards the city of Sravasti at the time people are getting ready to prepare the noon meal, you would see every householder bring his lens into the sunlight to kindle a fire. The quality of fire is not developed by means of the combining and conforming of lens and high noon and wormwood kindling. Why? Because as one holds out his lens to the heat of the sunlight in order to kindle a fire, does the fire come from the glass, or does it come from the wormwood fiber that the concentrated heat kindles, or does the fire come

from the sun, Ananda? If the fire comes from the sun and kindles the wormwood fiber, why is not the whole forest of wormwood trees kindled also? If it comes from the lens and is hot enough to kindle the wormwood, why is the lens itself not burnt? As it is, there is no appearance of fire until your hand holds out the lens between the sun and the fiber. Again, Ananda, think carefully. Here are certain conditions that being present, fire arises; you are holding a lens in your hand, the sunlight is coming from the sun, the wormwood fiber has grown from the ground, but where does the fire come from, and how does it sojourn here? It can not be said that the fire comes from nowhere.

"Ananda, why is it that you still remain in ignorance that the intrinsic nature of fire is the real emptiness, while the intrinsic nature of space is the real fire-essence. In the Womb of Tathagata, both fire and space abide in freshness and purity and permeate everywhere throughout the universes and are being manifested freely and perfectly corresponding to the inheritance and accumulation of Karma by the conscious activity of sentient beings. You should therefore know, Ananda, that wherever people in this world hold out lenses (or bore hard dry wood into hard dry wood) fire may be kindled, and as fire may be kindled everywhere, there is the place where fire originates. Fire obeys, and fire is everywhere. Given conditions, it arises, but it is not the conditions that manifested it; nor does it rise spontaneously by reason of its own nature, because if it did, all would be in flames everywhere and forever. And if everywhere and forever nothing but fire could be seen, in combination with propitious circumstances that assist in making fire appear, what would it signify? Would it not signify that this universal fire was Universal Mind? Or if everywhere and forever nothing but water was seen, in combination with propitious circumstances that assist in making water appear, what would it signify? Would it not signify that this universal water was Universal Mind? But as it is, there's water here, fire there, because they are conditional manifestations dependent and put-together, and the two work and transform each other continually, like boiling water being poured over ice and just as continually being frozen again. And so action continues. But people of this world being ignorant of this, and by regarding fire as being manifested by causes and conditions, or spontaneously by means of its own nature, have become bewildered. Whereas, all of their false presuppositions and prejudices are simply the discriminations made by their own mental consciousness, and are merely figurative words having no meaning in reality.

"Ananda, as to fire, it is as though it was the nature of filth, the essential nature of filth is neither disgusting nor not disgusting, but who is going to face that reality?"

Ananda said: "Pray tell us, my Noble Lord, about the wind-element."

The Blessed One replied: "Why is wind a reflection, Ananda? Does it fit the case to question whether a reflection is permanent or impermanent?

"Let us consider the nature of wind. It has no visible substantiality and it has no permanency either when in motion or in quietness. For instance, whenever I move my hand near your face a little breeze from it blows on your face. What think you, Ananda, does this little breeze that responds freely and with perfect accommodation to the motion of my hand, like a reflection in a mirror come from my hand, or does it come from the air-space between my hand and your face? If it came from my hand, then when my hand is resting quietly in my lap where is the breeze? If it comes from the space of air, why do your scarfs hang motionless? Moreover, as the nature of space is permanent, the breeze if it comes from space should be blowing constantly. As there is no breeze does it mean that there is no space, either? As the breeze comes and goes, what is its appearance as it comes and goes? If it comes and goes then space would have its disappearances and appearances, deaths and rebirths, and could no longer be called space. If it is called space, how can it give out wind from its emptiness? If the breeze that is felt on one's face, comes from that face, then the breeze would be always felt there. What originates the breeze and just where does it come from? The breeze is asleep in emptiness, I can rouse it up by motion of my hand, but the origin of the breeze is not in the motion of my hand because is that where the originality of the breeze is to be returned when my hand is still? My hand is empty space and breeze is everywhere. If wind comes out everywhere, where can be the particular locality that is the origin of wind?

"Ananda! Why is it that you still remain in ignorance that in the Realms of Tusita which are beyond arbitrary conceptions of any kind whether the conceptions are about existence or non-existence, the intrinsic nature of wind is the real emptiness, while the intrinsic nature of space is the real wind-essence.

"And the same with space, which is to be regarded as the Fifth Great Element. Ananda, the nature of space possesses no form because it is crystal clear emptiness which we have reduced in our mortal minds to something that abides between somethings that appear to exist, such as stars and they are imaginary separation. The only way that space is manifested to our senses is by colors, the infinitesmal dust in the sky reflects sunbeams and we see blue, for instance. But space itself is only another one of our arbitrary conceptions, and there is not even such a thing as 'empty space' which would imply that separative things like planets, and imaginary things like the walls of a hole, truly existed in the first place.

"When you dig a well, dirt by the pound becomes space in the ground. For instance, Ananda, when there is one well dug, space is manifested to the limit of one well, and when all the ten quarters of the universes become empty, the space of emptiness is manifested all throughout the universes, also. If the space of emptiness is perfectly permeating everywhere throughout the ten quarters of the universes, then where can the space of emptiness be seen and located? But the world is all in ignorance and bewilderment because they have always regarded the space of emptiness as being manifested by causes and conditions such as the removal of objects, like the removal of dirt from a hole, while all the time the intrinsic nature of space is what is always there, real Enlightenment, and the intuition of Essence is the real emptiness. The appearance of the dirt does not hide the emptiness of space, the emptiness of space does not annihilate the appearance of the dirt. You should carefully observe as to whether space comes out from some unseen place, and pray, what's unseen?—or whether it comes in from something seen outside, and we already know that perception of sight is false and fantastic!—or does it neither come out from or come into?

"Ananda, you are ignorant that within Tathagata's Womb, space and the Essence of Enlightenment are ever in freshness and purity, permeating everywhere throughout the phenomenal universes, and are being manifested freely and perfectly in correspondence to the amount of Karma accumulated by the conscious activity of sentient beings.

"Space, together with earth, water, fire, and wind, are to be regarded as the Five Great Elements, whose essential nature is perfect, and all-in-unity, and all alike belonging to the Tathagata's Womb, and all alike devoid of deaths and rebirths.

"Ananda, I mention the Tathagata's Womb, and the Tathagata (Suchness-As-Is), to concentrate your attention on the bright and perfect Mystery beyond all our conceptions and pitiful teachings. Even as I speak to you about the Tathagatas who ever abides beyond coming and going, teaching and nonteaching, still my words are like a finger pointing at the truth and not to be taken as the truth itself. The True Essence, the Truth, has actually by nature remained unrevealed because of the false imagination of existence itself.

"The Truth has only been mentioned by the Buddhas because, being an explanation of bondage to and emancipation from that figure of speech 'Existence,' it is also just a figure of speech.

"So to speak, the Truth is so vast that it can afford to say that there is no Truth.

"There is neither Truth or Non-Truth, there is only the essence. And when we intuit the essence of all, we call it Essential Mind.

"Ananda, the Sixth Great Element is perception. We think of it as being either perception of seeing, of hearing, of smelling, of tasting, of touching, or of thinking, but it is intrinsically One Perception and by nature pure.

"The six sense-organs that seem to divide perception into six kinds of perception, are like six knots that seem to divide one silk handkerchief into six kinds of knotty appearances, but as soon as we undo the knots we see it is still only one pure handkerchief like one pure perception no matter how many knots may be tied or untied in it.

"Wherever there are eyes, and the arbitrary conception of brightness and darkness, and sights, there will arise Perception of sight; just as, wherever flints are struck, there will arise the spark of fire.

"Wherever there are ears, and the arbitrary conception of motion and stillness, and sounds, there will arise Perception of sound.

"Wherever there is the nose, and the arbitrary conception of passability and impassability, and smells, there will arise Perception of smell.

"Wherever there is the tongue, and the arbitrary conception of changeability and unchangeability, and flavors, there will arise Perception of taste.

"Wherever there is the body, and the arbitrary conception

of contact and separation, and touching, there will arise the Perception of touch.

"Wherever there is the brain, and the arbitrary conception of appearance and disappearance, and thoughts, there will arise Perception of thought.

"Like the other great elements, Perception does not have its place of origination in causes and conditions and combinations, but responds to them and obeys and is conducted through them as through a tube: nor does it have its own nature, because it appears in only a limited way, as, for instance, Perception of thought, which is limited and impermanent.

"But the Essence of Perception is perfect and in one unity with the empty perfect Essence of earth, water, wind, fire, and space (the other five) in the Womb of Tathagata, devoid of re-births and deaths.

"The intrinsic nature of Perception is the real emptiness; the intrinsic nature of space is the real perception-essence.

"Where does Perception come from and how does it sojourn here? Perception obeys and perception is everywhere.

"The Seventh Great Element is Consciousness. Ananda, let us look at those springs and pools in the beautiful Jetavana Grove given to the Brotherhood by the pious merchant Anatha-pindika. Conciousness abides in tranquillity permeating every-where throughout the phenomenal worlds and embracing all ten quarters of the universes without number, but at the contact of our eyes and springs and pools, satori it appears in the form of consciousness of the perception of sight of springs and pools.

"Why do you still raise questions as to its locality of existence? Consciousness obeys, and Consciousness is everywhere, for where does this Consciousness go when there are no sights and thoughts?

"Ananda, naturally, you have never known that within your Womb of Tathagata the essential nature of Consciousness is enlightening and intelligent, that is, for instance, it neither is conscious of perception of sight of spring and pools, nor not-conscious, it is conscious of the Dharma of No-Things. Ananda, are you going to say that that rock and that pool are two different things? It were better if you were to say that each one is a Buddha, and that we only need one Buddha because all things are No-Things, and that all things are therefore Buddhas. This is the Diamond Knowledge, all the rest is knowledge about ripples and balloons. This enlightened intuition is your true Essence of Consciousness and it is like the intrinsic nature of space."

Thereupon Ananda and all the assembly, having received this wonderful and profound instruction from the Lord Tathagata and having attained to a state of perfect accommodation of mind and perfect emancipation of mind from all remembrances, thinking and desires, became perfectly free in both body and mind. Each one of them understood clearly that the mind can reach to all the ten quarters of the universes and that their perception of sight can reach to all the ten quarters also. It was just as clear to them as though it was a blade of grass held in their hand. They saw that all the worldly phenomena was nothing but their own wonderful, intelligent, original Mind of Enlightenment, their physical bodies begotten from their parents seemed like specks of dust blowing about in the open space of the ten quarters of the universes. Who would notice their existence? Their physical body was like a speck of foam floating about on a vast and trackless ocean, with nothing distinctive about it to indicate from whence it came, and if it disappeared whither it went. They realized very clearly, that they, at last, had acquired their own wonderful Mind, a Mind that was Permanent and Indestructible.

Therefore the whole assembly with palms pressed together in adoration made obeisance to their Lord Buddha in greatest respect and sincerity as though for the first time they had realized his transcendent worth.

Then they together chanted, praising the glory of their Lord Tathagata and voicing their sincere devotion to him.

The Buddha concluded the instruction by saying: "Ananda, with respect to your own body, as you look on it, it bewilders you to hear that causes and conditions acting in combination are neither the cause of it nor not the cause.

"Ananda, you owe the appearance of your body in this world neither to your father's seed, or your mother's womb, or to nutriment alone: neither do you owe the appearance of your body to none of them, if so you would not be here; neither do you owe the appearance of your body to all three combined, seed and womb and nutriment. Your body owes its appearance to that which was already waiting in tranquillity and purity and emptiness, and which responded to the action of seed and womb and nutriment, and if it had not been for the action it would not have responded and appeared but would have remained as it is in the Pure Mind of Enlightenment. Your body is only proof of the fact that if seed is placed in a womb and nutriment provided, a body appears. Why? If your father's seed had not been placed in your mother's womb and nourished, nothing would have appeared but would have remained as it is in the Mind of Enlightenment. You say your body owes its appearance to your father's seed? How is it a man's seed inside of him does not sprout some child? Owes its appearance to your mother's womb? Then women's wombs would spring such bodies everywhere and forever, instead of having to wait for insemination, as it is. Owes its appearance to nutriment? Then you could produce bodies like these by feeding nutriment in the sea or on a bed of stones. Does not owe its appearance to any of these? Without seed, womb and nutriment, your body would not have appeared. Owes its appearance to all three together combined? The appearance of your body is owing to the Seven Great Elements that the combination of birth drew in to activity and combined and transformed, but these elements do not originate in the combination, but beyond the combination in their own One and Tranquil Essence. Your body is only a conductor of mysterious elements abiding everywhere, which accommodate perfectly its genesis and continuation and respond its way, but the elements themselves are undisturbed and un-born and not liable to destruction when the body is thrown on the funeral fire and burned.

"A body only proves that the insemination of a woman by a man, assists in the appearance of bodies, that is, the activity of rebirth, and the mystery is that the body is really mind-made and really independent of its own bodiness! That is why your body, being a mere figure of speech, can neither be said to be existent or non-existent, neither caused nor not-caused, because in the Essential Mind of Enlightenment which is awake beyond conception no such discrimination is held. As I look at your body, I realize it is just a visionary bloom in the void, it has no hold on Reality. Where do the elements come from, that give your body its bodiness, and how do they sojourn here? Ananda, they come from everywhere; this is a Sea of Mystery.

"Ananda, your body is like a thought, it is an impermanent form materializing awhile in the permanent essence of Mind. The essence of the thought and the essence of the Mind are the same, naturally, but the form is just a passing fancy which is completely ignored in Mind's Essence of Omniscience which we call the Womb of Tathagata for purposes of teaching, it is neither considered as existent or inexistent. Who would notice it?—as a mirror the vain child, Ananda?"

The assembled holy men, each one feeling like a man who had inherited a magnificent palace through the munificence of a heavenly King but could not take possession of it without first passing through the door of Enlightenment into the Bright Room of Perfect Wisdom, hard to achieve, bowed down at the feet of the Great Lord and, with Ananda as their natural spokesman, beseeched him for further sacred instruction, with regard to the actual starting-point for their devotion and their disciplinary practice, wishing each one surely to attain the intelligence and insight of the Lord Buddha.

Ananda concluded by saying: "We pray thee, my Noble Lord, to show us how to get rid of all entangling conditions and thus to encourage all of us who are still practicing Arhats to concentrate our minds on the right path."

The Blessed One, in tones of tender and sorrowful compassion, and placing his hand kindly on Ananda's head, replied:-

"Ananda, within your body there is an element of hardness, of Earth; there is an element of fluidity, of Water; there is an element of warmth, of Fire; and an element of breathing and motion, the element of Wind. The body is in bondage to these Four Great Elements, and these four bonds divide your tranquil, mysterious, intuitive, enlightening Mind into such divisions as the sensations and perceptions of seeing, hearing, tasting, smelling and touching, and of the following conceptions and discriminations of thought, that cause your enlightened Mind to fall into the corresponding five defilements of this evil world from its beginning and will continue to do so to its end.

"What are these five defilements, Ananda? What is their nature? Consider the difference between fresh, pure spring water, and such substances as dust, ashes and sand. If these are mixed, the water becomes opaque and dirty. It is just the same with the five defilements and the mind.

"Ananda, when you look into the vast space that stretches beyond the universe, the nature of space and the nature of the perception of sight do not interfere with each other and mingling together there is no boundary line to limit their individuality. But if there is only empty space, with no suns nor planets in it, then space loses its substantiality. No objects means that there is no conception such as space. Also, the conception of sight looking into space with nothing to see, loses its sensibility. But as there is this false phenomenon of two arbitrary conceptions—suns and planets moving in space, and the false perception of sight, all interwoven together,—so there are all the uncounted false appearances of differences in the universes.

"As you don't clearly and continuously realize that it is all a hallucination made of the mindstuff, ignorant wrinkles on the surface of it, you go on being a victim of this first defilement of Individuation, of 'making-out' seeing and perceiving which is the basis of ignorance.

"This is the first defilement, the Defilement of Discriminating Ignorance.

"Next, having perceived the mass of phenomena as being a jumble of differences, your processes of the mind mingling with the processes of the body become interwoven together into the false imaginations that are the second defilement where you note details and develop erroneous views concerning the differences of form, not realizing that the substance of one form is not different from the substance of another. Is there any difference between the substance of light and the substance of shadow?

"This is the second defilement, the Defilement of Form.

"Again, having developed a notion of form and details and in accordance with the conscious processes within your mind, and including your pure intuition, you conceive a desire or aversion for these different forms.

"This is the third defilement, the Defilement of Desire.

"Again, having developed the desire based on the notion of discriminated form, and note how one leads to another, you grasp at these things, not realizing what they are, objective illusions. Your mind is continually in a process of change from morning to night, and every time your thoughts change, you seek to manifest and perpetuate them by some sort of creative activity in the terrestrial world. And every time your actions, conditioned by your Karma, take form, they transform sentient lives also. These interwoven false imaginations bring sentient beings to grasping the things they desire. Desire poses as a friend, but in secret 'tis an enemy.

"This is the fourth defilement, the Defilement of Grasping.

"Finally, your perceptions of seeing, hearing, touching, thinking, smelling and tasting have no difference in their nature in the pure Essence of Mind, and are mutually accommodating, but when they are placed in opposition to one another revealing abnormal differences, they become mutually incompatible. Thus there arise internal and external conflicts, which, although imaginary and mind-only, lead to weariness, suffering, growing old and decrepitude.

"This is the fifth defilement, the Defilement of Decrepitude, Old Age, Disease and Death.

"Ananda, why do you suffer decrepitude from grasping at

the desire for some form that you should not have individuated in the first place?

"Ananda! Whenever during the course of your practice of holy meditation some vagrant thought obtrudes itself in your tranquil mind, run it backwards through the wringer of the five defilements, see it clearly, survey its effect of decrepitude destroying your tranquillity and all because of grasping at it, which is because of desire, which is because of form, which is because of discriminating ignorance. And the same with evil passions when they arise in your Mind in the stress of action, run the passion through the wringer of the five defilements, ask yourself, "Ananda, why do you allow yourself to fall into suffering and decrepitude by grasping at the desire to discriminate and ravish this form which is only an imaginary idea in Reality?"

"Ananda! If you wish your sense perceptions and conscious understanding to be in harmony with the permanent joy of the Tathagata's natural purity, you must first pull up these roots of death and rebirth which have been surreptitiously planted by these five kinds of defilements, namely, the defilements of discriminating ignorance, of form, of desire, of grasping, of decrepitude, and then begin the practice of concentration of your attention on the pure and essential mind of non-death and non-rebirth.

"Yes, Ananda, sit thee in tranquillity, under a tree or anywhere you might be, and close your eyes, and breathe gently and serenely, loosen the knot in your stomach, relax, rest, remember the Light, and think: 'This is the pure and essential Mind of non-death and non-rebirth, this shining essence is the Holy Reality, all else is a dream.'

"For when it is realized that there is nothing born, and nothing passes away, then there is no way to admit being and non-being, and the mind becomes quiescent. It is by means of your quiescence of mind that you are able to transmute this false mind of death and rebirth into the true and clear Intuitive Mind and by so doing, to realize the primal, enlightening and intuitive Essence of Mind. You should make this your starting point for practice.

"If you wish to tranquillize your mind and restore its original purity, you must proceed as if you were purifying a jar of muddy water. You first let it stand until the sediment settles to the bottom when the water will become pure, which corresponds with the state of mind before the defilements of the evil passions had troubled it. Then you carefully strain off the pure water which is the state of the mind after the five defilements of ignorance, form, desire, grasping, decrepitude, have been wholly removed. When the mind becomes tranquillized and concentrated into perfect unity, then all things will be seen, not in their separateness, but in their unity wherein there is no place for the evil passions to enter, and which is in full conformity with the mysterious and indescribable purity of Nirvana.

"Ananda! Do not for a moment think that because accidental and momentary thoughts are stopped, that the Mind stops also.

"It is just like the accidental and momentary sound of the gong when I strike it, when the sound dies away and there is perfect silence, has your ability to hear died away?

"It is not right for you to say that if your thinking is separated from arbitrary conditions such as appearance and disappearance, death and rebirth that the perception of thinking would have no essential nature of its own.

"All sentient beings, from beginningless time, have always hankered after beautiful sights and musical sounds and blissful feelings and exquisite flavors and lovely fragrances, filling their thinking minds with thought after thought and causing it to be always active, thinking that the Mind should be used, never realizing that it is beyond the using; never realizing that by nature it is pure, mysterious, permanent, and Void Divine, thus causing them, instead of following the path of permanency, to succumb to the five defilements and follow the current of transitory deaths and rebirths. Consequently there has been life after life ever recurring and ever filled with contaminations, impermanency and suffering.

"Like so many dead birds on the ground, Ananda, are these lives, these forms. Does it fit the case to question whether a form is joyful or not?

"Ananda, if you could only learn to get free from this bond-age to deaths and rebirths and from this fear of impermanency, and learn to concentrate your mind on its true and permanent nature of Permanency, which is an inconceivable activity that has nothing to do with time or haste because it belongs to He-Who-Is-Already-Good (Sugata), then the eternal Brightness would illumine you and all the individualized and discriminated perceptions of objective phenomena, sense-organs, false imagi-nations, self and not-self, would vanish, for the phenomena of the thinking brain-mind are only empty and transitory things, the differentiated emotions of your mortal consciousness are only passing phenomena. If you can learn to ignore these two fundamental illusions—deaths and rebirths and the fear of impermanency—and hold fast to the Permanency that the Eye of Dharma perceives, which until now you thought to be a trivial and unreal instinctive vision that had no room in a busy world of facts, but now you see as the only reality in-deed and the rest puppet-shows and racing up and down the Buddha-mountain, then you need have no fear of failure, Ananda, no fear indeed in the attainment of Supreme and Sacred Enlightenment."

Suddenly it seemed that all the trees of the Jeta Park, and all the waves lapping on the shores of its lakes, were singing the music of the Dharma, and all the intersecting rays of brightness were like a net of splendor set with jewels and over arching them all. Such a marvelous sight had never been imagined by the assembled holy devotees and held them all in silence and awe. Unwittingly they passed into the blissful peace of the Diamond Samadhi, that is, every one immediataly listened to the intense and mysterious roar of silence, the entire multitude of twelve hundred and thirty three, and upon them all there seemed to fall like a gentle rain the soft petals of many different colored lotus blossoms—blue and crimson, yellow and white— all blending together and being reflected into the open space of heaven in all the tints of the spectrum. Moreover, all the differentiations of mountains in their minds, and seas and rivers and forests of the Saha-suffering world blended into one another and faded away leaving only the flower-adorned unity of the Primal Cosmos. In the center of it all, seated on pure lotus, they saw the Tathagata, Already-Thus, the Pearl and the Pillar of the world.

Thereupon Manjusri addressed his Lord Buddha, saying:- "Blessed Lord! Since my Lord has descended from the Angel Realms to this reincarnating suffering world, he has helped us most by his wonderful enlightening Teaching. At first we receive this Teaching through our sense of hearing, but when we are fully able to realize the Teaching, it becomes ours through a Transcendental Faculty of Hearing. This makes the awakening and perfecting of a Transcendental Faculty of Hearing of very great importance to every novice. As the wish to attain Samadhi deepens in the mind of any disciple, he can most surely attain it by means of his Transcendental Organ of Hearing. At first, it is only on occasions, or in enclosed places, or in breezeless mid-watches of night, when all creatures seem to be asleep, and the deep resonant hush of silence fills the ear, that the novice can concentrate his attention on this Intrinsic Sound of Reality which is the absence of sound, the Hearing of the Emptiness Sublime. He recognizes it at once as the Eternal Hearing that has been going on in his own pure and Essential Mind of non-death and non-rebirth since beginningless time. My Lord, in the silence he hears a teaching going on! Later on, he learns to hear it everywhere and under all conditions.

"For many a kalpa—as numerous as the particles of sand in the river Ganges—Avaloki-Tesvara Buddha, the Hearer and Answerer of Prayer, the Bodhisattva of Tenderest Compassion, has manifested the Sacred Teaching Without Words in all the Buddha-lands of the ten quarters of the universe and has acquired Transcendental Powers of boundless Freedom and Fearlessness and has vowed to emancipate all sentient beings from their bondage and suffering. How sweetly mysterious is the Transcendental Sound of Avaloki-Tesvara! It is the pure Godly Sound. It is the subdued murmur of the sea-tide setting inward. Its mysterious Sound brings liberation and peace to all sentient beings who in their distress are calling for aid; it brings a sense of permanency to those who are truly seeking the attainment of Nirvana's Peace.

"While I am addressing my Lord Tathagata, he is hearing, at the same time, the Transcendental Sound of Avaloki-Tesvara. It is just as though, while we are in the quiet seclusion of our Dhyana practice, there should come to our ears the sound of the beating of drums and if our minds, hearing the sounds, are undisturbed and tranquil, this is the nature of perfect accommodation.

"The body develops feeling by coming in contact with something, and the sight of eyes is hindered by the opaqueness of objects, and similarly with the sense of smell and of taste, but it is different with the discriminating brain-mind. Thoughts are rising and mingling and passing. At the same time it is conscious of sounds in the next room and sounds that have come from far away. The other senses are not so refined as the sense of hearing; the nature of hearing is the true reality of Passability.

"The essence of sound is felt in both motion and silence, it passes from existent to non-existent. When there is no sound, it is said there is no hearing, but that does not mean that hearing has lost its preparedness. Indeed! When there is no sound, hearing is most alert, and when there is sound the hearing nature is least developed. If any disciple can be freed from these two illusions of appearing and disappearing, that is, from death and rebirth, he has attained the true reality of Permanency.

"Even in dreams when all thinking has become quiescent, the hearing nature is still alert. It is like a mirror of enlightenment that is transcendental of the thinking mind because it is beyond the consciousness sphere of both body and mind. In this Saha world, the doctrine of intrinsic, Transcendental Sound may be spread abroad, but sentient beings as a class remain ignorant and indifferent to their own Intrinsic Hearing. They respond only to phenomenal sounds and are disturbed by both musical and discordant sounds.

"Notwithstanding Ananda's wonderful memory, he was not able to avoid falling into an evil way. He has been adrift on a merciless sea. But if he will only turn his mind away from the drifting current of thoughts, he may soon recover the sober wiseness of Essential Mind. Ananda! Listen to me! I have ever relied upon the teaching of the Lord Buddha to bring me to the indescribable Dharma Soul of the Diamond Samadhi. Ananda! You have sought the secret lore from all the Buddha-lands without first attaining emancipation from the desires and intoxications of your own contaminations and attachments, with the result that you have stored in your memory a vast accumulation of worldly knowledge and built up a tower of faults and mistakes.

"You have learned the Teachings by listening to the words of the Lord Buddha and then committing them to memory. Why do you not learn from your own self by listening to sound of the Intrinsic Dharma within your own Mind and then practicing reflection upon it? The perception of Transcendental Hearing is not developed by any natural process under the control of your own volition. Some time when you are reflecting upon your Transcendental Hearing, a chance sound suddenly claims your attention and your mind sets them apart and discriminates them and is disturbed thereby. As soon as you can ignore the phenomenal sound the notion of a Transcendental Sound ceases and you will realize your Intrinsic Hearing.

"As soon as this one sense perception of hearing is returned to its originality and you clearly understand its falsity, then the mind instantly understands the falsity of all sense perceptions and is at once emancipated from the bondage of seeing, hearing, smelling, tasting, touching and thinking, for they are all alike illusive and delusive visions of unreality, and all the three great realms of existence are seen to be what they truly are, imaginary blossoms in the air.

"As soon as the deceiving perception of hearing is emancipated, then all objective phenomena disappear and your Intuitive Mind of Essence becomes perfectly pure. As soon as you have attained to this Supreme Purity of Mind-Essence, its Intrinsic Brightness will shine out spontaneously and in all directions and, as you are sitting in tranquil meditation, the mind will be in perfect conformity with Pure Space.

"Ananda! As you return to the phenomenal world, it will seem like a vision in a dream. And your experience with the maiden Pchiti will seem like a dream, and your own body will lose its solidity and permanency. It will seem as though every human being, male and female, was simply a manifestation by some skillful magician of a manikin, all of whose activities were under his control. Or each human being will seem like an automatic machine that once started goes on by itself, but as soon as the automatic machine loses its motive power, all its activities not only cease but their very existence disappears.

"So it is with the six sense organs, which are fundamentally dependent upon one unifying and enlightening spirit, but which by ignorance have become divided into six semi-independent compositions and conformities. Should one organ become emancipated and return to its originality, so closely are they united in their fundamental originality, that all the other organs would immediately cease their activities also. And all worldly impurities will be purified by a single thought and you will attain to the wonderful purity of perfect Enlightenment. Should there remain some minute contamination of ignorance, you should practice the more earnestly until you attain to perfect Enlightenment, that is, to the Enlightenment of a Tathagata.

"All the Brothers in this Great Assembly, and you too, Ananda, should reverse your outward perception of hearing and listen inwardly for the perfectly unified and intrinsic sound of your own Mind-Essence, for as soon as you have attained perfect accommodation, you will have attained to Supreme Enlightenment.

"This is the only way to Nirvana, and it has been followed by all the Tathagatas of the past. Moreover, it is for all the Bodhisattva-Mahasattvas of the present and for all in the future if they are to hope for Perfect Enlightenment. Not only did Avaloki-Tesvara attain Perfect Enlightenment in long ages past by this Golden Way, but in the present, I also, am one of them.

"My Lord enquired of us as to what expedient means each one of us had employed to follow this Noble Path to Nirvana. I bear testimony that the means employed by Avaloki-Tesvara is the most expedient means for all, since all other means must be supported and guided by the Lord Buddha's Transcendental Powers. Though one forsake all his worldly engagements, yet he cannot always be practicing by these various means; they are special means suitable for junior and senior disciples, but for laymen, this common method of concentrating the mind on its sense of hearing, turning it inward by this Door of Dharma to hear the Transcendental Sound of his Essential Mind, is most feasible and wise.

"Oh Blessed Lord! I am bowing down before my Lord Tathagata's Intrinsic Womb, which is immaculate and ineffable in its perfect freedom from all contaminations and taints, and I am praying my Lord to extend his boundless compassion for the sake of all future disciples, so that I may continue to teach Ananda and all sentient beings of this present kalpa, to have faith in this wonderful Door of Dharma to the Intrinsic Hearing of his own Mind Essence, so surely to be attained by this most expedient means. If any disciple should simply take this Intuitive Means for concentrating his mind in Dhyana Practice on this organ for Transcendental Hearing, all other sense organs would soon come into perfect harmony with it, and thus, by this single means of Intrinsic Hearing, he would attain perfect accommodation of his True and Essential Mind that does not pass away."

Then Ananda and all the great assembly were purified in body and mind. They acquired a profound understanding and a clear insight into the nature of the Lord Buddha's Enlightenment and experience of highest Samadhi Meditation Ecstasy. They had confidence like a man who was about to set forth on a most important business to a far-off country, because they knew the route to go and to return. All the disciples in this great assembly realized their own Essence of Mind and purposed, henceforth, to live remote from all worldly entanglements and taints, and to live continuously in the pure brightness of the Eye of Dharma.

Thereupon the Lord Buddha, in conclusion, advised the following rules of Discipline to those who most surely wished to attain to the stage of Great Wise Being (Bodhisattva-Mahasattva) in this life.

1. Concentrate the Mind
2. Keep the Precepts
3. Practice Dhyana

"Concentrate the mind" means to stay wise and pure, continuously, to see things as they are and not to be fooled into believing in their respective "realities" and so to cease to grasp at them. It is like a man who wakes up in the middle of the night to the supreme and final truth and nods with satisfaction, saying, "Everything is the same thing." He wakes up from a dreamless sleep of perfect unified void in which there was no such conception as "perfect unification" and he sees that all created things are the same as emptiness, that they are surface manifestations in a perfectly empty sea of Single Reality, that they are not individuated parts but one whole Is-ness, all the Same.

"Keep the precepts" means to adhere strictly to the four principal rules of purity, so that by so doing the disciple being free from the intoxicants, becomes free from suffering, and therefore he is free from Sangsara and all its polluting, tristful, illusionary conceptions of death and rebirth. The Precepts are based on kindness to all living creatures, and are self-purifying. "O Monk, empty this boat!!! if emptied, it will go quickly; having cut off passion and hatred, thou wilt go to Nirvana."

The Four Precepts are:-

T
H
 E

  F
   O
    U
     R

      P
       R
        E
         C
        E
       P
      T
     S

1. Wake up, cease sexual lust, sexual lust leads to multiplicity and strife and suffering.

2. Wake up, cease the tendency to unkindness toward others, unkindness is the murderer of the life of wisdom.

3. Wake up, cease greediness and stealing, you should look upon your own body as not being your own but as being one with the bodies of all other sentient beings.

4. Wake up, cease secret insincerity and lying, there should be no falsehood in your life, there is no hiding anything in a shattering dewdrop.

"Practise dhyana" means to make it a regular practice to meditate in holy trance so as to attain to Samadhi Meditation Ecstasy and Samapatti Spiritual Graces and Powers which are the states of liberation from this Sangsaric world as pointed out by all the Mighty Awakened Ones in the past, in the present, and to come.

As the Lord Buddha finished his instruction, recorded in the Surangama Sutra, there was great rejoicing in the hearts of all those present, bhikshus and bhikshunis, lay disciples of both sexes, Great Wise Beings, Practising-Buddhas, Saints, Arhats, and newly converted mighty Kings. All made sincere and humble obeisance to the Buddha and departed with grateful and joyful hearts.

Devadatta became notorious in later days by attempting to found a new sect of his own with severer and stricter rules than those prescribed by the Buddha. He acquired great skill in magic of a worldly kind, including hypnotism. This he practiced on the young Prince Ajatasutru, son of pious Bimbisara, bringing him to a determination to murder his father. Becoming king of Magadha, Ajatasutru had a special monastery built for Devadatta. Devadatta prevailed and induced the new king to help him oust Gotama from the leadership of the Sangha Brotherhood, claiming that old age had overtaken the Blessed One.

Buddha, ignoring this folly, said of his cousin:- "He is as one who seeks to pollute the ocean with a jar of poison."

Seeing that his plot to wrest power from the Blessed One had failed, and not realizing that the Blessed One did not think in terms of "power" or "weakness," Devadatta proceeded to plot against his life. Bands of cutthroats were set up to kill the Lord, but they were converted as soon as they saw him and listened to his preaching, won over by his loving and dignified bearing. The rock hurled down from the Gridhrakuta hill to hit the Master split in two, and luckily both pieces passed by without doing him much harm. A drunken elephant was let loose on the royal highway just at the time the Blessed One was coming along that path; the savage and spiteful behemoth, beholding Buddha, came to himself at once, and bending, became docile in his presence, for, like St. Francis of Assisi, the Blessed One had a strange power over animals. With lotus hand the Master patted the head of the beast, even as the moon lights up a flying cloud, and said:-

"The little elephant breaks down the prickly forest, and by cherishing him we know that it can profit men; but the cloud that removes the sorrow of the elephant old-age, this none can bear. You! swallowed up in sorrow's mud! if not now given up, lust, anger and delusion will increase yet more and grow."

The elephant called Dhanapalaka, his temples running
with pungent sap, and who is difficult to hold,
does not eat a morsel when bound; the elephant longs
for the elephant grove.

—DHAMMAPADA

To his disciples the Buddha said:- "Silently I endured abuse
as the elephant in battle endures the arrow sent from the bow;
for the world is ill-natured. They lead a tamed elephant to battle,
the king mounts a tamed elephant, the tamed is the best among
men, he who silently endures abuse. Mules are good, if tamed,
and noble Sindhu horses, and elephants with large tusks; but he
who tames himself is better still."

Thus the Blessed One was equally minded to Devadatta, the
conspirator, and to Rahula, his own worthy son. Devadatta was
regarded by the members of the Order as a typical "fool." Each
enlightened Bhikshu understood and believed that Devadatta
will come again as a Buddha, knowing that all things are the
same in Supreme Reality of Anuttara-Samyak-Sambodhi (Highest
Perfect Wisdom).

Young King Ajatasutru, seeing the dismal failure of his
foolish heretical hero, suffering greatly from the pangs of con-
science, sought peace in his distress by going to the Blessed One
and learning the way of salvation.

Jealousy rose in the hearts of other heretical leaders owing to the Master's massive popularity and the gifts which pious lay-people were bestowing on the disciples of the Buddha. These leaders sought to drag the Blessed One's reputation through the mud and discredit him in the eyes of the people. A false nun belonging to a heretical sect was persuaded to accuse the Blessed One of adultery before the entire assemblage. Chincha's callous lie was exposed. The heretics made another attempt to blast the Master with calumny. They got a woman called Sundari to spread a rumor that she had passed the night in the bed-chamber of the Teacher. This slander was also repudiated, but meanwhile the conspirators had Sundari killed by a band of drunks bribed for the purpose. The vicious fools threw the corpse in the bushes near the monastery in the Jeta Park. The heretics wanted it to look like an attempt on the part of Gotama's followers to cover up a scandal, and that they had lost their heads in so doing. Consequently loud voices were raised demanding legal steps to be taken against the Lord Buddha. But the drunken murderers fell out and began fighting in the tavern, accusing one another and so the secret leaked out. They were arrested that night and brought before the king's tribunal. On questioning, they admitted their guilt and revealed the names of their employers. On still another occasion, Narasu writes:- "The heritics instigated Srigupta to take the life of the Master by poisoning his food and misleading him into a pit of fire, but by pity and calm forgiveness the Holy One saved Srigupta from spite and crime and showed how mercy conquers even a foe, and thus he taught the rule of forgiveness sublime, freeing his followers from the woe of the world."

Elated and believing, perceiving the serenity, the moral earnestness, the sweet reasonableness of the Master, more and more disciples joined the Brotherhood. Of his Twelve Great Disciples, 500 years before Christ and His Twelve, the Blessed One said: "Save in my religion the Twelve Great Disciples, who, being good themselves, rouse up the world and deliver it from indifference, are not to be found."

One day while staying in the southern district the Buddha visited the Brahman village of Ekanala. A wealthy Brahman, cane in hand, was overseeing his laborers who were sweating with oxen in the field. The Buddha, begging-pot in hand, calmly approached the harassed and vexatious squire. Some of the humble laborers came to the Blessed One and made obeisance with palms pressed together, but the millionaire was annoyed and rebuked the Holy One with these words: "O you Quiet One, I plough and sow, and having ploughed and sown, I eat; it would be better if you were in like manner to plough and sow, and then you would also have food to eat."

"O Brahman," replied the Blessed One, "I too plough and sow, and having ploughed and sown, I eat."

"But," said the Brahman, "if you are a farmer, where are the signs of it? Where are your bullocks, the seed, and the plough?"

Then the Teacher answered: "Faith is the seed I sow; devotion is the rain that fertilizes it; modesty is the plough-shaft; the mind is the tie of the yoke; mindfulness is my ploughshare and goad. Truthfulness is the means to bind; tenderness, to untie. Energy is my team and bullock. Thus this ploughing is effected, destroying the weeds of delusion. The crop that I harvest is the Ambrosial fruit of Nirvana, and by this labor all sorrow is brought to an end."

Whereupon this Brahman, ignoring his servant who stood beside him, himself poured milk-rice into a golden bowl and handed it to the Lord Buddha saying: "Eat, O Gotama, the milk-rice. Indeed, thou art a farmer; for thou, Gotama, accomplishest a ploughing, which yields the fruit of immortality."

To the assembled pious clan of Likkhavi princes the Blessed One said:- "To gain the end of wisdom first banish every ground of 'self'; this thought of 'self' shades every lofty aim, even as the ashes conceal the fire, treading on which the foot is burned.

"Pride and indifference shroud this heart, too, as the sun is obscured by the piled-up clouds; supercilious thoughts root out all modesty of mind, and sorrow saps the strongest will.

"As I am a conqueror amid conquerors, so he who conquers 'self' is one with me.

"He who little cares to conquer 'self,' is but a foolish master; beauty, of earthly things, family renown and such things, all are utterly inconstant, and what is changeable can give no rest of interval.

"This right apprehension once produced then there is deliverance from greedy desire arising from 'self,' for a false estimate of excellency produces a greedy desire to excel, while a false view of demerit produces anger and regret, but this idea of excelling and also of inferiority both destroyed, the desire to excel and also anger are destroyed.

"Anger! how it changes the comely face, how it destroys the loveliness of beauty!"

As when a snake subdued by charms glistens with shining skin, so the Likkhavi warriors were appeased by the Blessed One's words and prospered in peace in their lovely valley. They found their joy in quietness and seclusion, meditating only on religious truth.

"What monk, O monks, adds to the glory of Gosingam Wood?" spoke the Buddha to Sariputra, to Maudgalyayana, to Ananda, to Anuruddha, to Revata, and to Kasyapa, on a cloudless night wafted with fragrance in the heavenly Wood. "It is the monk, O monks, who, having turned from his begging round and partaken of his meal, sits down with crossed legs under him, body upright, and brings himself to a state of recollectedness, 'I will not rise from this spot,' he resolves within himself, 'until freed from clinging, my mind attains to deliverance from all Bane.' Such is the Monk, O monks, who truly adds to the glory of Gosingam Wood."

The truth is older than the world, heavier than history, a greater loss than blood, a greater gift than bread.

In his 80th year as Nirmanakaya Buddha walking upon the terrace of the earth, yet like all of us a spiritual ghost in the Divine Ground, he suddenly said: "The time of my complete deliverance is at hand, but let three months elapse, and I shall reach Nirvana."

Tathagata, seated beneath a tree, straightaway was lost in ecstasy, and willingly rejected his allotted years, and by his spiritual power fixed the remnant of his life.

Buddha rising from out of his ecstasy announced to all the world:-

"Now I have given up my term of years: I live henceforth by power of faith; my body like a broken chariot stands, no further cause of 'coming' or of 'going,' completely freed from earth, heaven and hell, I go enfranchised, as a chicken from its egg.

"Ananda! I have fixed three months to end my life, the rest of life I utterly give up; this is the reason why the earth is greatly shaken."

Cried Ananda: "Have pity! save me, master! perish not so soon!"

The Blessed One replied: "If men but knew their own nature, they would not dwell in sorrow. Everything that lives, whatever it be, all this is subject to destruction's law; I have already told you plainly, the law of things 'joined' is to 'separate.'"

And as Ananda wept in the dark wood, the Blessed One spoke to him these sad, true words:-

"If things around us could be kept for aye, and were not liable to change or separation, then this would be salvation! Where can this be sought?

"That which you may all attain I have already told you, and tell you, to the end.

"There is love at the center of all things and all things are the same thing. Svaha! I am resolved, I look for rest. The one thing needful has been done, and has long been done.

"Adoration to all the Tathagatas, Sugatas, Buddhas, perfect in wisdom and compassion, who have accomplished, are accomplishing, and will accomplish all these words of mystery. So be it!

"Ananda, prepare quietly a quiet place, be not moved by others' way of thinking, do not compromise to agree with the ignorance of others, go thou alone, make solitude thy paradise; the Brotherhood of the Gentle Eyes, the white-souled tranquil votaries of good, will support thee.

"The mind acquainted with the law of production, stability, and destruction, recognizes how again and once again things follow or succeed one another with no endurance. The wise man sees there is no ground on which to build the idea of 'self.'

"The wise man had nothing to do with form before his birth, has nothing to do with form now, shall have nothing to do with form after he dies, free from anxious thoughts about relationships. And how will he die, knowing that being and not-being of his form are the same?

"Ananda, weep not. My purpose is to put an end to the repetition of birth of form. Unfixed, unprofitable, under the nailer, without the marks of long endurance, constantly blowing and changing and agonized with restraint and restlessness, all things are in a branch of torment because of form.

"Unconsoled, all things that are formed, come to ultimate decay.

"Receive the Law as it explains itself."

To the Likkhavis of Vaisali who came with grievous faces after having heard of his decision to die, the Blessed One said:-
"In ancient days the Rishi Kings, Vasishtha Rishi, Mandhatri, the Kakravartin monarchs, and the rest, these and all others like them, the former conquerors, who lived with strength like Isvara (God), these all have long ago perished, not one remains till

now; the sun and moon, Sakra himself, and the great multitude of his attendants, will all, without exception, perish; there is not one that can for long endure; all the Buddhas of the past ages, numerous as the sands of the Ganges, by their wisdom enlightening the world, have all gone out as a lamp; all the Buddhas yet to come will also perish in the same way; why then should I alone be different?

"I too will pass into Nirvana; but as they prepared others for salvation, so now should you press forward in the path, Vaisali may be glad indeed, if you should find the way of rest!

"The world, in truth, is void of help, the 'three worlds' not enough for joy—stay then the course of sorrow, by engendering a heart without desire.

"Give up for good the long and straggling way of life, press onward on the northern track, step by step advance along the upward road, as the sun skirts along the western mountains."

In his last preaching tour the Master came to the town of Pava, and there in the house of Chunda, the blacksmith, he had his last repast. The Blessed One understood that the pork offered by Chunda was not fit to eat and very bad; Sukara-maddava, it has been established, a kind of poisonous truffle; he advised his monks not to touch it and in conformity with the Buddhist rule of accepting all alms from the faithful no matter how poor and lowly, he ate it himself. After this he became mortally ill of dysentery and moved to Kusinagara in the eastern part of the Nepalese Terai.

To Ananda he said: "Between those twin Bala trees, sweeping and watering, make a clean space, and then arrange my sitting-mat. At midnight coming, I shall die.

"Go! tell the people, the time of my decease is come: they, the Mallas of this district, if they see me not, will ever grieve and suffer deep regret."

He warned his disciples never to accuse Chunda, the blacksmith, of being responsible for his death but rather to praise him for bringing Nirvana nigh to the Leader of men.

To the Mallas who came in tears he said: "Grieve not! the time is one for joy. No call for sorrow or for anguish here; that which for ages I have aimed at, now am I just about to obtain; delivered now from the narrow bounds of sense, I leave these things, earth, water, fire, and air, to rest secure where neither birth or death can come.

"Eternally delivered there from grief, oh! tell me! why should I be sorrowful?

"Of yore on Sirsha's mount, I longed to rid me of this body, but to fulfil my destiny I have remained till now with men in the world: I have kept this sickly, crumbling body, as dwelling with a poisonous snake; but now I am come to the great resting-place, all springs of sorrow now forever stopped.

"No more shall I receive a body, all future sorrow now forever done away; it is not meet for you, on my account, for evermore, to encourage any anxious fear.

A sick man depending on the healing power of medicine, gets rid of all his ailments easily without beholding the physician.

"He who does not do what I command sees me in vain, this brings no profit; whilst he who lives far off from where I am, and yet walks righteously, is ever near me!

"Keep your heart carefully—give not place to listlessness! earnestly practice every good work. Man born in this world is pressed by all the sorrows of the long career, ceaselessly troubled—without a moment's rest, as any lamp blown by the wind!"

In his last moments the Blessed One received a monk Subhadra, a heretic, showed him that the world is cause-produced and that by destruction of the cause there is an end, a bowing-out, explained to him the Noble Eightfold Path, and converted him to the true faith of the Brotherhood of the Tender and Loving and Sad, announcing, "This my very last disciple has now attained Nirvana, cherish him properly."

The Blessed One gave final instructions under the trees, sitting up to do so, as Ananda, out of his mind with despair, longed to place the frail sad head of his Lord in his lap to support and protect him from pain's mindless indecency in this hour of death.

Said the Lord Buddha: "Keep the body temperate, eat at proper times; receive no mission as a go-between; compound no philteries; abhor dissimulation; follow right doctrine, and be kind to all that lives; receive in moderation what is given: receive but hoard not up; these are, in brief, my spoken precepts.

"Adore thy good-will, for they who do kind and hopeful good pay me most honor, and please me most.

"As in the last month of the autumn rains when the sky is clear and the clouds are gone, the great sun climbs the vault of heaven, pervading all space with his radiance, so good-will glows radiant above all other virtues; yea, it is as the morning-star.

"The black toad that dwells within his heart, the early waker disenchants and banishes.

"Give not way to anger or evil words towards men in power. Anger and hate destroy the true Law; and they destroy dignity and beauty of body.

"As the mongoose immune from the poison of the snake, even so the monk living amid hate and anger with tender heart.

"From the 'desiring-little' we find the way of true deliverance; desiring true freedom we ought to practice the contentment of 'knowing-enough.' For the rich and poor alike, having contentment, enjoy perpetual rest.

"Do not become insatiable in your requirements, and so through the long night of life gathering increasing sorrow. Many dependents are like the many bands that bind us; without this wisdom the mind is poor and insincere.

"Ever and ever have these pitiful, frightened selves gulped through to death, changing dreams miraculously, returning in ignorant new skin of babes; like trees,—arms, heaviness, blear peace.

"The poor wretches, deficient in wisdom and conduct, lapsed into the mundane whirl, retained in dismal places, plunged in affliction incessantly renewed. Fettered as they are by desire like the yak by its tail, continually blinded by sensual pleasure, they do not seek the Buddha, the mighty one; they do not seek the Law that leads to the end of pain.

"Hearing my words and not with care obeying them, this is not the fault of him who speaks."

Near midnight in the silence of their brotherly woe the Blessed One said to his disciples: "Maybe it is from reverence to the Teacher that ye keep silence: let us rather speak as friend to friend."

Anuruddha stepped forth and said: "O Blessed Lord, passed the sea of birth and death, without desire, with nothing to seek, we only know how much we love, and, grieving, ask why Buddha dies so quickly?"

And, "O my heart is joined to him!" cried Pingiya.

The Honored Elder Brother of Mankind said: "What think you, Brothers? Which is greater, the floods of tears which, weeping and wailing you have shed upon this long way, ever and ever again hastening towards new birth and new death, united to the undesired, separated from the desired, this, or the waters of the Four Great Seas?

"Long time, Brothers, have you suffered the death of a mother, for long the death of a father, for long the death of a son, for long the death of a daughter, for long the death of brothers and sisters, the loss of goods, the pangs of disease.

"There are some whose eyes are only a little darkened with dust, and they will perceive the truth.

"As a bird whom sailors loosed to discover land, came back when it failed to find it, so having failed to find the truth thou has returned to me.

"As thinking nothing of herself, a mother's love enfolds and cherishes her only son, so now through the world let thy compassion move, and cover everyone.

"Even robbers will we permeate with stream of loving thought unfailing; and forth from them proceeding, enfold and permeate the whole wide world with constant thoughts of loving-kindness, ample, expanding, full of divine approval, joyously free from enmity, free from all suspicious fear. Yea, verily, thus, my disciples, thus must you school yourselves.

"Having arrived at the farther shore and reached Nirvana, do you not guide others to its safety?"

Ananda rose and sang his mournful song:-

"For five-and-twenty years on the
Exalted One
   I waited, serving him with
loving thoughts
   And like his shadow followed
after him.
   When pacing up & down the
Buddha walked,
   Behind his back I
kept the pace always;
   And when the Law was being
taught,
   In me knowledge grew, &
understanding.
   But O he dies, now
he dies!
   And I am one yet with
work to do,
   A learner with a mind
not yet matured,

The flower of my pity has
not opened
    And now the Master
breaks my heart & dies,
    He, the Holy One, Awakened
Perfect in Wisdom & Compassion,
    He, the Incomparable Trainer
of men,
    He, the Morning-Star,
Love's White Dove
and Suckling Lamb,
    He, Milk of Rain and
Transcendental Pity,
    the Chariot of Spotless
White, the Child, the Lotus King,
    the Angel in Our Mind,
He dies, O now he dies
And leaves me mortal dimness
    in the unimaginable brilliance
    of the Void!"

Surrounding the Sala grove were younger monks and lay
people who had realized that what this man taught was not only
a verity, but the very hope of their salvation, because for the first

time they had recognized in his words, which expressed the radiant confidence of his discovery, the truth that made of slaves free men, and of castes and classes brotherhood. But now because of the oncoming death of the temporary form of his body they were afraid, wise lambs affrighted by the assurance of the ignorant lion Death.

To them and to Ananda and to ease and purify their minds the Buddha said:- "In the beginning things were fixed, in the end again they separate; different combinations cause other substances, for there is no uniform and constant principle in nature. But when all mutual purposes be answered, what then shall chaos and creation do! the gods and men alike that should be saved, shall all have been completely saved! Ye then! my followers, who know so well the perfect law, remember! the end must come; give not way again to sorrow.

"Use diligently the appointed means; aim to reach the home where separation cannot come; I have lit the lamp of wisdom, its rays alone can drive away the gloom that shrouds the world. The world is not forever fixed! You should rejoice therefore! As when a friend, afflicted grievously, his sickness healed, escapes from pain. For I have put away this painful vessel, I have stemmed the flowing sea of birth and death, free forever now, from pain! For this you should exult with joy!

"Now guard yourselves aright, let there be no remissness! That which exists will all return to nothingness!

"And now I die.

"From this time forth my words are done, this is my very last instruction."

Entering the Samadhi ecstasy of the first Dhyana meditation, he went successively through all the nine Dhyanas in a direct order; then inversely he returned throughout and entered on the first, and then from the first he raised himself and entered on the Fourth Dhyana, the Dhyana of Neither Joy nor Suffering, utterly pure and equal, the original and eternal perfect essence of Mind. Leaving the state of Samadhi ecstasy, his soul without a resting-place forthwith he reached Pari-Nirvana, complete extinction of the form after it has died.

The moon paled, the river sobbed, a mental breeze bowed down the trees.

Like the great elephant robbed of its tusks, or like the ox-king spoiled of his horns; or heaven without the sun and moon, or as the lily beaten by the hail, thus was the world bereaved when Buddha died.

Only in Nirvana is there joy, providing lasting escape, for to escape from the prison, was why the prison was made.

The diamond mace of inconstancy can overturn the mountain of the moon, but only the diamond curtain of Tathagata, the iron curtain of the mind, can overwhelm inconstancy! The long sleep, the end of all, the quiet, peaceful way is the highest prize of sages and of heroes and of saints.

Voluntarily enduring infinite trials through numberless ages and births, that he might deliver mankind and all life, foregoing the right to enter Nirvana and casting himself again and again into Sangsara's stream of life and destiny for the sole purpose of teaching the way of liberation from sorrow and suffering, this is Buddha, who is everyone and everything, Aremideia the Light of the World, the Tathagata, Maitreya, the Coming Hero, the Walker of the terrace of earth, the Sitter under Trees, persistent, energetic, intensely human, the Great Wise Being of Pity and Tenderness.

The noble and superlative law of Buddha ought to receive the adoration of the world.

———— THE END ————